Happy Mo

Mom and Dad

250 WAYS TO CONNECT WITH YOUR FAMILY

MELODIE WEBB

DESERET
BOOK

SALT LAKE CITY, UTAH

Library of Congress Cataloging-in-Publication Data

Webb, Melodie M.
    250 ways to connect with your family / Melodie M. Webb.
    p.   cm.
    ISBN 1-57008-914-0 (pbk.)
    1. Mormon families—Religious life.   2. Family—Religious aspects—Mormonism.
3. Family life.   4. Interpersonal relations.   5. Social values.   I. Title: Two hundred
fifty ways to connect with your family.   II. Title.

BX8643.F3W43   2003
248.4—dc21   2003005414

Printed in the United States of America   72076-7046
Publishers Printing, Salt Lake City, UT

10   9   8   7   6   5   4   3   2   1

This book is lovingly dedicated to
David, Taylor, Sara, Carlie, and Lauren Webb

President Spencer W. Kimball prophesied:

"The time will come when only those who believe deeply and actively in the family will be able to preserve their families in the midst of the gathering evil around us."

(*Ensign,* November 1980, 4)

CONTENTS

ACKNOWLEDGMENTS

No work could ever be complete without expressing gratitude for the people who made it possible in the first place. A heartfelt *thank you* to:

- ♡ My loving Heavenly Father whose precious gift of inspiration gave me this opportunity to testify of him, his love, and his Son.

- ♡ My family: My husband, David, who owns my heart and allows me to so completely experience love in this lifetime, and to look forward to the exciting reality of forever. My children, Taylor, Sara, Carlie, and Lauren, who make every day worth the effort, and give me the honor and privilege of being their mom. Their support and encouragement are everything to me.

  Also, to my ancestors whose devotion to family is so much a part of who I am. And to my parents, who have always believed in me and taught me the meaning of loving my family, past, present, and future.

- ♡ My friends: My new friend, Jana Erickson, whose time and belief in me have been invaluable. My travel companions (through my husband's business), whose examples to me are far beyond what they can possibly imagine. The friends of my youth, who have offered enthusiasm, feedback, and motivation. And to Mary, who convinced me I had something worth sharing.

THE GIFT

Your family is a precious gift from God. *Your* family, with its quirks, its dynamics, its personalities. Your family has limitations and weaknesses, but more importantly, it has possibilities and strengths. Your family has a purpose and a part in a loving Heavenly Father's plan.

As you hear the word *family,* many different images may come to your mind. You may be single, divorced, or married, with or without children. You may think of a loving parent, a beloved ancestor, a special child, or a young grandchild. You may feel great joy at the sound of the word or you may feel sorrow or anxiety. Whatever your situation, whatever your season of life, you likely feel strong desires and concerns for the people that you call family. Your heart is "turned" to them.

Ancient prophets lovingly saw our day. They saw your family and they saw mine. They saw the latter days and both the great and the terrible things that would occur. Modern prophets as well have added their voices to prepare us for what lies ahead. We have been warned of a danger threatening our families: a growing sense of emotional and spiritual disconnection. But we have also been promised a solution. If we work to plant in the hearts of the children the promises made to the fathers (see D&C 2:1–3), then our families can grow closer together emotionally and spiritually and we can be connected forever as a family, past, present, and future.

As parents, we have two main duties that will help us connect our family: we must teach the gospel and we must show love. Helaman describes the main source and subject of our teaching and loving: "And now, my sons, remember, remember that it is upon the rock of our Redeemer, who is Christ, the Son of God, that ye must build your foundation; that when the devil shall send forth his mighty winds, yea, his shafts in the whirlwind, yea, when all his hail and his mighty storm shall beat upon you, it shall have no power over you to drag you down to the gulf of misery and endless wo, because of the rock upon which ye are built, which is a sure foundation, a foundation whereon if men build they cannot fall." (Hel. 5:12.) We learn from this scripture that there are three guarantees or promises that we can "plant" or "build" in our family's hearts: Jesus Christ is a *sure* foundation, the devil *will* send mighty trials and temptations our way, and if we build upon the Rock, we *cannot* fall.

Heavenly Father has not given us just the *responsibility* for this "planting." He has given us the *power* to make it happen. He has commanded us to teach and to love the way he does, he has given us the Rock upon which to build, and he has given us the promises he has made before to our fathers. He has also given us eternal principles that have a binding effect upon our family and our testimony. He has given us so many gifts to help us connect with our family, and we will be blessed with his love and power if we truly seek him as we make the effort.

It doesn't matter what current circumstances you find yourself in, or what your current definition of family is. This book is written with your family in mind. When you read these pages, if you feel that something doesn't apply to your current circumstances, remember that eternal principles have a connection to your everyday life and are a constant in a changing world. The principles will still be available and true always. Heavenly Father has ways of blessing us beyond our expectations in times of great abundance or in times of need. It is possible to connect with your family, even in these perilous times. It is worth it. Stay close to our loving Heavenly Father, and as your heart is turned to your children and your children's hearts are turned to you, you will find the answers for your family that you have been seeking.

Remember, your family doesn't matter just to you. Your family matters to the Lord. His choicest blessings will be with you as you allow him and his eternal principles to guide you in connecting your family.

1
CENTER YOUR HOME LIFE IN JESUS CHRIST

"And we talk of Christ, we rejoice in Christ,
we preach of Christ, we prophesy of Christ,
and we write according to our prophecies,
that our children may know to what source
they may look for a remission of their sins."

2 Nephi 25:26

Center Your Home Life in Jesus Christ

1. Teach your family about the life and teachings of Jesus Christ and the importance they have in your lives.

Teach about Christ in family night, in Sunday discussions, in conversations around the dinner table, and in heart-to-heart talks. Teach about him by sharing stories, songs, and prayers with children of all ages. Teach through the kinds of books you buy, the kinds of magazines you subscribe to, the kinds of goals you aspire to. Teach by example on a daily basis.

2. Express your own personal testimony that Jesus Christ is your Savior.

Express your testimony often. Be a witness of Christ *every time you have the opportunity* to express your testimony to your family, both publicly and privately. A simple, quiet expression that you know he is real, that you have placed your faith in him, that you are grateful for his light in the darkness, is a witness or testimony of him and does not require eloquence, microphones, or "amens."

3. Speak his name with great reverence and love at the end of every prayer.

Never mumble the name of Christ, skip over it, or miss the opportunity to use descriptive words such as *Savior, Friend, Brother, Beloved, Loving, Kind, Merciful, Gracious, Compassionate,* in connection with his name. Read *His Holy Name* by Elder Dallin H. Oaks for greater understanding.

4. Encourage a personal relationship with Christ.

Encourage your family to internalize and personalize their feelings for the Savior. Encourage them to think of him *every time* they partake of the sacrament. Display the *New Era* poster of a hand holding a sacrament cup and the words "Take it personally." Encourage children to ask, "What would he want me to do?" and to pray in Jesus' name for answers to their questions.

5. Apply the basic principles of the Atonement—repent and forgive.

Nothing has more of a cleansing and healing effect than these two principles. Teach your family the importance of repentance and forgiveness. Help them to understand these principles and how to use them in their lives and in their relationships with other people. Start by saying "I'm sorry" when you do something wrong. Be quick to forgive even when forgiveness has not been sought. Use repentance and forgiveness as family home evening topics often, always reminding your family who the Giver of the gift is.

6. Motivate your family with visual reminders of Christ.

Place a picture of the Savior in every child's bedroom and in the main gathering place of your home. Reinforce the Savior's example of obedience by wearing CTR rings. Consider making a sign that says: "Christ is the center of our home." Plant a garden with reminders of him such as dogwood trees, bleeding hearts, lilies, or forget-me-nots. Show through these visual symbols that all things testify of him.

7. Take maximum advantage of special dates and events to remember Christ.

Christmas, Easter, and every Sunday, reverence the Savior through expressions of gratitude, lessons about his life, bearing testimony, respectful dress, and worshipful attitudes. Let your family know the high value you place on partaking of the sacrament and help them to understand the significance of this ordinance. Take the opportunity to focus your family's celebrations of Christmas and Easter on Christ, rather than on the secular symbols of the holidays. *A Christ-Centered Easter,* by Janet and Joe Hales, is an excellent resource for commemorating the true meaning of Easter.

8. Teach the Atonement throughout the year in family home evening.

Don't talk about the Atonement just at Easter time, and then leave the subject for another year. Teach about the Savior and his sacrifice several times a year, so that elements of his life and Atonement will be a focus in your family and expressions of testimony about Christ will be consistent and constant. Help your family understand that the Atonement is for now, for always. It doesn't apply just to the end of this life, and it isn't just for "everyone else." No matter who we are, the Atonement applies to each of us personally.

Teach the Atonement often. We will spend our whole lives growing in understanding about this sacred subject, but the basic principles can be taught early, and appreciated and loved by everyone.

9. Hold a family testimony gathering.

Consider having a family testimony gathering where each member of the family has the opportunity to share, to discuss, to bear witness of him. Testimonies may be shared vocally or expressed silently, perhaps by recording them in a journal. It doesn't even need to be an official meeting with an "amen" at the end. Make the gathering a comfortable place to share these important feelings. Sharing testimony develops testimony, strengthens testimony, and solidifies testimony.

10. Walk the walk, and talk the talk, of a true Christian.

It has been said that "the more Christlike we become, the more like Christ we become." Show by example and deed that you know who he is and what he did for you, and that you love him enough to follow his teachings. Let his love shine in your eyes and become the guiding principle in how you treat others. Follow the words of the apostle Paul when he said, "Be thou an example of the believers." (1 Tim. 4:12.) Discuss as a family ways to exemplify the teachings of Christ. Discuss that one way people can "take his name in vain" is to be called by his name, as we are through baptism, and then to not live according to what we know.

SUMMARY

The Proclamation on the Family teaches us that "Happiness in family life is most likely to be achieved when founded upon the teachings of the Lord Jesus Christ."

Teach the atonement of Jesus Christ without hesitation or apology. The Atonement is truth. It is real. Our eternal life and happiness depends upon our acceptance of the Savior and the gifts he gave to us through his divine sacrifice. Our happiness in this life depends upon our returning love *to* him.

The Atonement is the single most important event in history—in your history. Make it an important part of your daily life, and encourage your family to do the same. The principles of the Atonement need to be applied, taught, and lived in your home *with love.*

The life and teachings of the Savior are the key to happiness for you and your family. Make it a part of your plan to be a witness of Christ and to serve in his name. Follow the counsel of Nephi and bring Christ into all facets of your life and worship so that your "children may know to what source they may look for a remission of their sins." (2 Ne. 25:26.) Be a believer, an example, and a teacher of the Savior's life, teachings, and atonement.

2
RECOGNIZE GOD'S HAND IN ALL THINGS

"In nothing doth man offend God, or against none is his wrath kindled, save those who confess not his hand in all things."

Doctrine and Covenants 59:21

RECOGNIZE GOD'S HAND IN ALL THINGS

1. Pray with your children.

As you pray together each day, let your children hear you acknowledge God's hand in your family's life. Let them hear in your voice the love you have for him. Take this opportunity to outwardly recognize God's love for you.

2. Pray often yourself so that your children know that *you* acknowledge the Lord's hand in your life.

Let them "catch" you praying on your knees once in a while. Express to your children the comfort and peace you experience in relying on the Lord for help with problems. Speak often and reverently of him. Stand as a witness of him in all things, through word and example.

3. Acknowledge the personal nature of your relationship with God.

♥ Call him "My Heavenly Father."

♥ Call his Son "My Savior."

♥ When expressing love for your child, say, "My Heavenly Father loves me so much, he gave me you!"

4. Whenever life is going really well, express to your family that you know Heavenly Father is blessing you.

Joseph Smith observed that "men not unfrequently forget that they are dependent upon heaven for every blessing which they are permitted to enjoy." (*History of the Church,* 2:24.) Recognizing God's hand in his blessings to us, President Hinckley has told us: "Get on your knees and thank the Lord for his bounties. Cultivate a spirit of thanksgiving for the blessing of life and for the marvelous gifts and privileges you enjoy." (*Improvement Era,* Dec. 1964, 1092.)

5. Whenever life is really hard, express to your family that you know Heavenly Father is blessing you.

In the day-to-day challenges we face, a simple expression that you know Heavenly Father is aware of your needs, watching over you, and helping you to endure will help your children to understand he is there for the good days and the bad. In extreme cases of despair, read together the pleadings of Joseph Smith while he was imprisoned in Liberty Jail. (See D&C 121:1–6.) Then read and discuss the Lord's response to the Prophet Joseph. (See D&C 121:7–8, 25–29; D&C 122.)

6. Teach your family hymns and Primary songs that acknowledge God's hand in your lives.

♥ "My Heavenly Father Loves Me" (*Children's Songbook,* 228.)

♥ "I Need My Heavenly Father" (*Children's Songbook,* 18.)

♥ "I Am a Child of God" (*Children's Songbook,* 2.)

♥ "I Feel My Savior's Love" (*Children's Songbook,* 74.)

♡ "Count Your Blessings" (*Hymns,* 241.)

♡ "Lead, Kindly Light" (*Hymns,* 97.)

7. Teach your children that you know some things with your mind—and some things with your heart.

You may not be able to see God, but you can feel his love and his presence. A simple object lesson to teach this to your family would be to ask them to feel the wind. Can you see it? No, but you know it's there.

You could discuss with your family the story of Cathy, a 70-year-old devout Christian of another faith who became converted to The Church of Jesus Christ of Latter-day Saints. On the day of her conversion, she expressed this tender sentiment: "I have known about my Savior all of my life, but today I *felt* him for the very first time!"

Or share this story from Harold B. Lee:

"I once had a visit from a young Catholic priest who came with a stake missionary from Colorado. I asked him why he had come, and he replied, 'I came to see you.'

"'Why?' I asked.

"'Well,' he said, "I have been searching for certain concepts that I have not been able to find. But I think I am finding them now in the Mormon community.'

"That led to a half-hour conversation. I told him, 'Father, when your heart begins to tell you things that your mind does not know, then you are getting the Spirit of the Lord.'

"He smiled and said, 'I think that's happening to me already.'

"'Then don't wait too long,' I said to him.

"A few weeks later I received a telephone call from him. He said,

'Next Saturday I am going to be baptized a member of the Church, because my heart has told me things my mind did not know.'

"He was converted. He saw what he should have seen. He heard what he should have heard. He understood what he should have understood, and he was doing something about it. He had a testimony." (*Stand Ye in Holy Places,* 1974, 92–93.)

8. Teach your family personal reliance upon God, and that Heavenly Father will always be with them.

♡ Teach them that God lives. He is aware of us. He loves us.

♡ Read Matthew 10:29–31, and discuss as a family why nothing in the universe is more important to God than his children.

♡ Teach them that we need not be alone, ever.

♡ Create a visual reminder of Proverbs 3:6: "In all thy ways acknowledge him, and he shall direct thy paths."

♡ Teach your children to look to him in all things and seek answers through prayer.

♡ Help your children find guidance from his words in the scriptures.

♡ Teach your family that all we have comes from him.

♡ Encourage your children to pray with gratitude.

9. Teach your family that God's commandments are not restrictions or burdens; rather, they are gifts and protections.

Teach your family that while God always loves us and will always be with us, it is important that we be obedient in order to feel that love on a deeper level. Explain that Heavenly Father desires that we be happy in this life and in the life to come and that obedience to his commandments will give us that happiness. Discuss Alma 41:10, which says, "Wickedness never was happiness," and help them to understand that "wickedness" is "disobedience," so disobedience will never bring us happiness. In other words, if you want to be truly happy, obey God. As your family reaches milestones or confronts decisions in life, understanding that God's commandments were preparations for those times and not restrictions will help them to understand God's love on that deeper level. Teach them to obey these "rules for happiness" because they love God, not because they fear him—then they can fully experience his divine love because their hearts are turned to him. Teach your family to see God as the God of love that he is.

10. Literally stop and smell the roses, and recognize their Creator.

Find opportunities to show your children the beauty of God's creations—a glorious sunset, a budding tree, a newborn baby. Thank him for the beauty and bounty in your life.

SUMMARY

To know that there is a God, to know that he has a plan for you, is the greatest knowledge of all. To know that he is aware of your needs, and that he has given you what you need in order to return to live with him someday, gives purpose to your life.

To be able to recognize his hand, his efforts in your behalf, his immeasurable blessings, his love, is the most basic of our needs, and our desires. Know God. Know that he hears and answers prayers. Know that he has your best interests at heart. Feel it, recognize it, and give thanks for it! He is there, he keeps his promises, and his hand is at work in your life!

3
LOVE EACH OTHER DEEPLY— FROM THE HEART!

"A new commandment I give unto you, That ye love one another; as I have loved you."

John 13:34

Love Each Other Deeply—from the Heart!

1. Place the needs of your family above your own.

When the Lord admonished us to "lose" our lives for his sake, he added that by doing so we would "find" ourselves. (See Matt. 16:25.) Through latter-day prophets, we have been told that our greatest joys will be found in our families, and that the greatest work we will ever do will be within the walls of our own homes. (Gordon B. Hinckley, *Motherhood: A Heritage of Faith,* 1995, 12.) The little choices you make that communicate the priority you place on your family have great significance. There is sweetness in service. There is much love shown and felt in placing their needs above your own.

2. See your family as Heavenly Father sees them.

See them as being valuable just because they exist, just because they are. See the same potential in them, the same worth and the same value that he sees. See in them the same divine nature Heavenly Father has always intended for you to see.

3. Recognize each person of your family as an individual.

Each member of your family is a separate person, with his or her own needs, perspectives, disappointments, fears, dreams, and feelings. Love them enough to allow them their own identity. Children should not become a way to live out our own unmet dreams, to be a miniature of ourselves, or to wear as a trophy. Recognize your children for the worth of their spirits, the individuality of their lives, and the desired destiny their Father has for them. Recognize *your* place in helping it happen.

4. Love unconditionally.

This means there are no ifs, ands, or buts associated with your love. You place no condition on whether love will be there or not—not "If your grades are good, and you take out the garbage," or "I love you, but . . ." The closest we can come to loving as Heavenly Father loves is to love unconditionally. This gives new meaning to the commandment that we love one another as we have been loved. It doesn't mean we have to accept inappropriate behavior or not make rules that need to be followed. It simply means that love is not withdrawn or withheld for any reason or in any situation.

5. Make family love a priority.

Make no exceptions. Place a high value on loving one another, on being friends to each other, on accepting each other, and on recognizing the worth of each other. Never, ever establish "favorites": don't place the value of one above another, compare children, or establish greater pride in one than in another. No child deserves to come in second place. Each deserves to be loved for who they are, not whether they can measure up to something or someone else. Every soul is great in the sight of God (see D&C 18:10–11) and should be the same in the sight of parents and families as well. Your family will be more successful, as individuals and as a family, when each member feels personally loved, validated, valued, understood, and invested in by you as a parent and by their siblings.

6. Make communicating love a priority.

♥ Be a good listener. Listen to understand; listen to validate.

♥ Communicate to establish love, importance, and worth.

♥ Speak softly and in loving tones.

♥ Remove gossip from your conversations, and don't discuss your children's (or your spouse's) problems outside the home.

♥ Read Dr. Gary Chapman's *Five Love Languages* books for marriage, for teens, and for children. Concentrate on communicating love to your family in the "language" they are most likely to hear.

♥ Be sincerely committed to love.

7. Lovingly set boundaries.

In the same way that Heavenly Father gives his children commandments or principles to live by and allows us, without withdrawing his love, to experience the consequences of our choices, we need to set boundaries for our children.

Children need to understand the principles and rules they should live by in order to have the power to withstand life's battles. A lack of teaching those principles can be perceived as a lack of love. Curfews, limits, chores, and expectations are all expressions that you care. Enforce them as protections, not restrictions. Enforce them in love, not in anger. Establish consequences to your children's actions, both good and bad.

8. Remember "roots" and "wings."

Someone once said that two of the most important things we can bestow upon our children are "roots" and "wings." We desire and are obligated to give our children "roots"—a sense of establishment, being firmly planted and deeply rooted in things that provide anchor, stability, constancy, meaning, and purpose. At the same time, we want to give our children the ability to fly, to be self-sufficient, to grow, develop, perform, achieve, believe, and be successful, happy individuals. These "wings" will help them achieve their true potential. Love your family by helping them develop both roots and wings.

9. Cherish every day, every season.

Be careful not to "wish your children's lives away" to a time when they are old enough to take care of themselves. Be careful not to wish their lives *back* to when they were little. Love and cherish each time and season for what it is. Cherish the simple pleasures of growing, appreciate the sweetness of every stage of your children's lives.

10. Love as you would want to be loved.

Remember the maxim that much of what we learn of love, we learn at home. How you teach love is how you will receive love. How you teach love is how your children will give love. The impact of your example of love will continue for generations to come.

SUMMARY

Love is the grandest of human emotions. It is also the most essential of human needs. Let love for your family be a governing principle, as it is for our Heavenly Father. Everything the Father does, he does in love. His plan of happiness for his children is designed, instituted, and carried out in love. Love is the greatest motivator, and catalyst for change. Love is something we will take with us when we leave this earthly life.

Heavenly Father sent us to earth in families so that we could experience love on a scale akin to his parental love for his children. Nothing runs deeper or more constant than his abiding, divine love. It is our challenge and our privilege to learn and strive to emulate that kind of love.

4

MAKE YOUR HOME
A SACRED PLACE

*"Because our Father loves his children, he
will not leave us to guess about what
matters most in this life concerning where
our attention could bring happiness or
our indifference could bring sadness."*

Elder Henry B. Eyring
(*Ensign,* February 1998, 10)

Make Your Home a Sacred Place

1. **Base your family life on the teachings and principles of Jesus Christ.**
   - ♡ Live according to his principles and teachings.
   - ♡ Place pictures of him in your home.
   - ♡ Speak of him often with your family.
   - ♡ Reverence his name; speak it with respect.
   - ♡ Give thanks for him in your prayers.
   - ♡ Acquire great books of art and literature on his life.
   - ♡ Practice repentance and forgiveness as you teach your family about his life and Atonement.
   - ♡ Learn of him often in family home evening.
   - ♡ Love him as he has loved you.
   - ♡ Pray often and sincerely in his holy name in your homes.
   - ♡ Partake of the sacrament each week in sacrament meeting, using the power of renewing your covenants to carry you through everyday life. This weekly reminder will aid you in carrying that spirit into your home.

2. Place the highest priority on home and family.

♡ Let the merits of your family outweigh the merits of the world. Don't be distracted by things that entice but never really satisfy.

♡ Choose to spend *quality* time with your family rather than with trivial pursuits.

♡ Make choices that allow you more *quantity* time with your family (see chapter 11).

♡ Live so that you won't say at the end of your life, "I wish I had spent more time with my family."

♡ Tell your family they matter most to you.

♡ Through your actions, *show* that they matter most to you.

♡ Live so that people can say of you that you are a "family man" or a "family woman."

♡ Recognize how much your family contributes to your personal success in life. Give them credit for that success.

♡ Verbalize daily in individual and family prayer how grateful you are for your family, and how much you desire to serve them.

3. Make your home a sanctuary.

♡ Make a visual reminder of this saying: "Home is the definition of God." (Emily Dickinson.)

♡ Establish a place of refuge from the storms of life by letting family members know that they are needed and wanted in your home.

♡ Insist on acceptance of one another.

♡ Make eye contact, connecting as you talk lovingly.

♡ Keep your family's confidences.

♡ Let the decor of your home create a feeling of peace and tranquility.

♡ Be careful how you respond to situations. Think before reacting.

♡ Establish your home as a "no-war zone." Work out differences in a spirit of love and peace.

♡ Control your temper.

♡ Control the volume of your voice.

♡ Permit absolutely no abuse—physical or verbal.

4. Remember simple values.

We can learn some things from the Amish people. When they believe in a principle, they live it and are unconcerned about what "outsiders" think of them. They are simple and humble, and they shun any sign of pride.

Family is everything to the Amish. They believe it is the parents who will love the child through life and eternity, so their lifestyle reflects that belief and responsibility.

♡ Have a spirit of "family" about everything you do.

♡ Teach the gospel in your home.

♡ Don't place more emphasis on your church calling than your family. This does not mean that you shouldn't serve in the Church. It means that you should have an appropriate priority and focus.

♡ Attend church as a family.

♡ Establish religion as a lifestyle in your home.

♡ Live in an atmosphere of love and order, unity and contentment.

♡ Respect elders, and teach your family to do the same.

♡ Love your neighbor and his family.

♡ Keep things simple.

5. Set your home apart from the world.

♡ Consider your home a missionary training center, a place where all who dwell there will learn the gospel well enough to share it.

♡ Subscribe to all Church magazines. They could be the only magazines you need in your home.

♡ Display family portraits and pictures of your children in your home.

♡ Hang your children's artwork up for everyone to see.

♡ Try to keep your home clean, neat, and organized.

♡ Place a high value upon education.

♡ Limit the number of TV channels that come into your home. (Limit the size and number of television sets in your home as well.)

♡ Live more simply. Resist the urge to own every new thing that comes out, including designer clothes, electronics, and other toys or gadgets.

♡ Never put a TV, phone, or computer in a child's room.

♡ Make places in your home for your family to enjoy being together.

♡ Make a place for family members to quietly read or study.

♡ Have a family Bible or set of scriptures in a prominent place, and make sure they don't get dusty!

6. Recognize the inherent worth of each member of the family.

♡ Respect differences.

♡ Celebrate the "sameness" we all share. We are *all* children of God. We are *all* dependent upon our Savior. We *all* have good days and bad days. *All* of our souls are of worth to Heavenly Father.

♡ Value the opinions of your spouse and children.

♡ Forget the notion that "children should be seen and not heard."

♡ Consider your children's feelings before responding to them, and never disregard them.

♡ At a special family event, give everyone the "VIP treatment." Roll out a red carpet! Then continually make them feel important.

♡ Don't humiliate or embarrass a family member in front of others.

♡ Don't correct one of your children in front of their siblings.

♡ Explain to your children that the reason Satan works so hard on them is that they are worth his effort because they are so good! Then help them understand that they are worth far more to their Father in Heaven, and he has given them the power necessary to overcome!

♡ Display this scripture in your home: "Remember the worth of souls is great in the sight of God; for, behold, the Lord your Redeemer suffered death in the flesh; wherefore he suffered the pain of all men, that all men might repent and come unto him." (D&C 18:10–11.)

♡ Teach the plan of happiness in your home so that family members know who they are, why they are here, and where they are going.

♡ Celebrate each person on birthdays, "un-birthdays," special events or holidays, or any other day in between!

7. Create and maintain love in your marriage.

♡ To truly love your children, love their mother or father. Love each other as you would like to be loved!

♡ Value your marriage, and let your marriage strengthen your family.

♡ Strive for unity on decisions. Truly be a team.

♥ Go on dates with each other.

♥ Value your spouse's opinions and dreams.

♥ Show affection towards each other.

♥ Never talk negatively about each other to your children.

♥ Remind your children how lucky they are to have their father or mother.

♥ Support individual endeavors.

♥ Show that you honor and respect each other.

♥ Pray together as a couple.

♥ *Enjoy* each other and cherish the journey.

8. Hold family councils.

♥ Make decisions together.

♥ Establish consequences together.

♥ Discuss topics and events of importance.

♥ Give each member a voice in what makes the family tick and what matters most, respecting all viewpoints.

♥ Establish family rules.

♥ Decide on what to save for together.

♥ Discuss options for family vacations together.

♥ Give plenty of opportunity for leadership.

♥ Respect family members' need for privacy.

♡ Don't single anyone out for bad choices they have made.

♡ Get together often, and make it something your family actually looks forward to rather than something to dread.

♡ Serve good refreshments!

9. Get control of family finances.

Family finances can have a great impact on the atmosphere in a home. A house full of debt is also full of anxiety, stress, and worry.

♡ Pay your tithing.

♡ Live within your means. (*Beneath* the level of your means would be even better.)

♡ Teach your family the principles that govern financial freedom as opposed to financial bondage.

♡ Resist the urge to "keep up with the Joneses."

♡ Don't envy others or think that "the grass is greener on the other side of the fence."

♡ If you are in debt, get involved in an accelerated debt reduction program. (Do not confuse this program with a debt consolidation loan, or declaring bankruptcy. Accelerated debt reduction is a very different, very effective way of working through debt. See Elder Marvin J. Ashton's pamphlet "One for the Money," available at no charge through Church distribution centers.)

♡ Be disciplined about wants versus needs.

♡ Save money for a rainy day. Save money for a sunny day, too.

♡ Be generous in your fast offerings and other charitable contributions, even if it is a sacrifice.

♡ Remember: "You can't take it with you!" Don't obsess over money and material things.

10. Live by the admonition in Doctrine and Covenants 88:119.

"Establish a house"—or a home—that is

♡ "a house of prayer,

♡ a house of fasting,

♡ a house of faith,

♡ a house of learning,

♡ a house of glory,

♡ a house of order,

♡ a house of God."

SUMMARY

Prophets down through the ages have instructed us in the sacred nature of homes and families. In the October 2002 general conference, President Gordon B. Hinckley declared: "If we fail in our homes, we fail in our lives. No man is truly successful who has failed in his home." (*Ensign,* Nov. 2002, 100.) President Harold B. Lee declared: "The greatest work you will ever do will be within the walls of your own home." (*Teachings of Harold B. Lee,* 1996, 280.) And President David O. McKay said, "No other success can compensate for failure in the home." He also said, "Pure hearts in a pure home are always in whispering distance of Heaven." (Conference Report, Apr. 1964, 5.)

Any of these principles listed can have an effect on your family at any stage of their lives, and can help to comfort, aid, relieve, and heal some of the problems you may be facing.

"Only the home can compare with the temple in sacredness." (LDS Bible Dictionary, s.v. "temple," 781.) It is never too late (or too early) to strengthen your family by striving to make your home sacred. No home is perfect, or even in "top form" all of the time, but we can fill our homes with faith and hope and our testimonies of the Father and his Son. As we do, the Lord will magnify our efforts beyond our best dreams.

5

PRAY WITH ALL THE ENERGY OF HEART

"Pray unto the Father with all the energy of heart, that ye may be filled with this love . . . ; that ye may become the sons [and daughters] of God; that when he shall appear we shall be like him . . . ; that we may have this hope; that we may be purified even as he is pure."

Moroni 7:48

Pray with All the Energy of Heart

1. Remember "the simpleness of the way."

In 1 Nephi 17:41 Nephi reminded his murmuring brothers of the children of Israel's experience with the fiery serpents, sent by the Lord because the people had hardened their hearts. The Lord then prepared a way for them to be made well. To be healed, all they had to do was to look upon the brazen serpent. But "because of the simpleness of the way, or the easiness of it, there were many who perished."

The way is simple. The answers are not complex. The simple healing you are looking for may be found in prayer. Establish a house of prayer by praying as a family.

2. Remember your individual prayers.

Pray in the morning, at night, while driving carpools or shopping at the grocery store. Keep your heart continually drawn out to Heavenly Father in prayer. Pray that the Father's desires for your family will be fulfilled, rather than merely responding to the daily struggles of family life.

3. Pray by the side of your child.

When your children are young, kneel beside them and pray with them before they go to bed. As they become older, remind them to remember their prayers and offer to pray with them occasionally.

4. As your children experience problems or difficulties, encourage them to seek answers in prayer.

Share with your children appropriate personal experiences of times when you received answers from prayer. Encourage them to pray for guidance and help with the challenges they face. Offer to pray *for* them, and *with* them. Lovingly remind your children that he will answer, although not always in the way we expect.

5. Always offer a prayer of thanks for the food you eat.

President Joseph F. Smith said that "one of the greatest sins of which the inhabitants of the earth are guilty today is the sin of ingratitude." (*Gospel Doctrine*, 1939, 270.) Teach your children to give thanks and to remember those who have not been blessed with the abundance which they enjoy.

6. Open and close family meetings or personal interviews with prayer.

Set a pattern of approaching Heavenly Father in all things by having your children participate in prayers to begin and end family home evenings, family councils, and personal interviews.

7. Assign a member of the family to be "in charge" of family prayer.

Select a family member to lovingly remind your family when it is time for family prayer. Rotate the assignment between family members.

8. Display thoughts or scriptures about prayer in your home.

This is a subtle way to remind your family of the importance of prayer. You may wish to get a photograph or statue of a family in prayer to display in your home or to place in individual bedrooms.

9. Encourage fasting with prayer.

Teach your children the principle of fasting in connection with prayer. Look for appropriate times to have a family fast and remember to begin and end the fast with prayer, helping your family to understand the value of drawing nearer to God through fasting and prayer.

10. Pray with a purpose.

As a family, pray for specific things with gratitude and with wholehearted reliance upon Heavenly Father. Don't allow family prayers to become repetitive or meaningless, even when there is something you are praying for every single day. Pray *sincerely* with the desire to do his will and you will find meaning and purpose in your prayers.

SUMMARY

Prayer is recognition of our Heavenly Father. It is recognition that he is God, that he is our Father, and that we are his children. Prayer recognizes our need as families and individuals to communicate with him, to seek for his guidance, to give him thanks and praise. We need to pray always in a spirit of humility, understanding our complete and total reliance upon God. Pray with the knowledge that he knows better than you do. Pray to understand your mission, your purpose in his teachings, and the lessons you may learn from the trials you experience. Pray with submission and acknowledgment of your willingness to accept his will and his timing. Let him know

that you recognize how much you need him, that you know how much he loves you, and that you desire to serve him. Pray as though he were really listening—he is. Talk to him as though he is your best friend—he is. Pray for the strength and wisdom and understanding, the guidance, direction, and comfort that he, and only he, can give you.

6
LIVE WITH
FAMILY PURPOSE

"You know, brethren, that a very large ship
is benefited very much by a very small helm
in the time of a storm, by being kept
workways with the wind and the waves."

Doctrine and Covenants 123:16

Live with Family Purpose

1. Create a family purpose statement.

Knowing where you want to go will help you decide what really matters to your family. Call it a flight plan, or a mission statement, a "unity of purpose" agreement, or your "Family Articles of Faith." Every pilot needs to know where he is going before he takes over the controls of the airplane. It is important for your family to know *where* you are going so you can make plans to reach your destination.

2. Give everyone an opportunity to create a portion of your family purpose statement.

Let each family member have some ownership in your family purpose statement by being involved in its creation. In a successful family unit, every voice is valid and important. The family purpose statement should not be a statement of dictatorship by the parents. To be meaningful and effective, your family purpose statement should be a consensus, an agreement of what is important and of value to your family.

3. Include statements of love for Heavenly Father and his Son Jesus Christ.

Clearly identify for your family your understanding of the purpose of life. Developing personal relationships with Heavenly Father and Jesus Christ should be high on your list as a family purpose, a family effort, a family cause.

4. Focus on "We believe" declarations as you write your family purpose statement.

The Articles of Faith are a great example of "We believe" statements that help us understand what we believe and what our purpose is. Focus your own family's purpose statement on what your family holds to be true and important. Use positive, uplifting, purposeful statements that everyone can feel a part of.

5. Make sure your family looks both inward and outward as you create your plan.

Consider what each person can do individually to contribute to the whole. In other words, family members need to recognize their own role and unique contribution to the success of the family. In addition, look at ways that your family can have a positive impact on your community, your neighborhood, your city, your world.

6. Focus on issues relevant to your specific circumstances.

Make your statement unique to your own family. The age of your children will have a great impact on your mission statement. So will their individual personality traits. Don't copy a statement from someone else. Recognize the good you can do and the values you can teach by focusing on the individual strengths and weaknesses of your own family.

7. Have everyone in the family sign a formal document.

For the signers of the Declaration of Independence, their signatures were a symbol of their dedication, commitment, and belief in the statements contained in that document. Impress upon your family the meaning and importance of signing their names to your family purpose statement. Remember to date your family purpose statement as well.

8. Make amendments as necessary.

Circumstances and needs change with time. With your family's input, make specific adjustments as you go along. Use family council time, family home evening, or personal interviews with your children to evaluate progress or need for change. Make any changes or amendments together as a family.

9. Display your family purpose statement in your home.

Place your family purpose statement in an area where family members will notice it often and be reminded of their importance to the success of your family. Make copies for your children's journals or scrapbooks and for your own journal and family history album.

10. Use family mottoes as reminders.

Mottoes are short, easily memorized statements with clever words designed to remind family members of your family purpose. Mottoes can be an actual part of your family purpose statement, or they can be short phrases to help your children make choices that are in line with your family purpose. Family mottoes may be printed and carried in your child's scriptures, school backpack, or wallet as a reminder.

Create family mottoes as specific needs arise, or as you are inspired by current events. Here are some examples:

♡ President Hinckley's 6 Bs—Be grateful, Be smart, Be clean, Be true, Be humble, Be prayerful.

♡ Leave a place better than you found it.

♡ Stand your ground.

♡ Go the distance.

♡ Return with honor.

♡ Endure to the end.

♡ Stand for truth and righteousness.

SUMMARY

A family purpose statement will give your family direction, purpose, unity, and focus as you journey through life together. Establish your purpose together in a spirit of love, allowing each family member to have a voice. A family purpose statement should be a lifetime document that allows for changes in the seasons of each member's life. It should serve as a guide and direction that offers comfort, security, and a sense of belonging, with realistic goals that are achievable for each family member.

7
FOSTER
FAMILY UNITY

*"And he commanded them that there
should be no contention one with another,
but that they should look forward with one
eye, having one faith and one baptism,
having their hearts knit together in unity
and in love one towards another."*

Mosiah 18:21

Foster Family Unity

1. Do things together as a family.

It may seem like this is stating the obvious, but sometimes we need to be reminded. Take walks, run errands, play games, work together. Enjoy being together and go out of your way to create opportunities that will provide lasting memories for your family.

2. Create secret codes and passwords for your family to use.

These passwords can be used as a protection from strangers. A person would have to give the password before a child would get in their car or help them to find their dog, and so forth. Secret codes that only your family understands can be used to express love or pass messages to your children in crowded places or public settings, such as on an airplane, in a dark theatre, or during a long meeting.

An example of an easy secret code or password is to take the last four digits of your phone number and use the corresponding letters on the number keys as initials for a fun message. For example, you could use the numbers to represent a family purpose, or the initials of a family motto: 3883=ETTE="Endure to the End." A zero could represent how you "operate." A "1" could stand for unity—"we are one." The password could be a reminder of a family motto, or a special phrase to let your children know you believe in them.

3. Invent a special way to sign your family name.

This could become something that others will recognize as your signature on greeting cards, and so forth. You might use all of the initials of your first names, or sign it as "The John Smiths," or use some sort of special symbol each time you sign your name.

4. Make up a team name for your family.

Talk about "team spirit," "teamwork," "team rules." Take a photo with your family in matching T-shirts imprinted with your team name. Make a puzzle out of the photograph and discuss how every piece of the team is needed for it to work.

5. Take yearly family portraits.

Snapshots are just as good, but frame and display them prominently. These photos become a photographic record of your family through the years and can convey a sense of belonging.

6. Send a family Christmas card.

Include a family picture with it. Make sure it is from your whole family, not just the parents. Send it to friends who live nearby, as well as those far away. Send it to your children's friends' families, as well as your own friends and their families. Include the elderly in your neighborhood.

7. Give each family member their own picture of the family.

These pictures can be put on their bulletin boards, in their lockers, in their desk at school, or in their office at work. Include one of your family mottoes.

8. Display items around your home that suggest family unity.

Family portraits, items that include everyone's names, a family height chart, or things that say *we* or *our* on them are good examples.

Include the date your family was established (the year you were married), for example, "The Smith Family, est. 1963." It could be as elaborate as an engraved piece of furniture, or as simple as a family "graffiti board" on the wall inside of the garage.

9. Make creations that spotlight the different personalities that make up your family.

Create family projects with names, pictures, or specific likenesses of family members. Here are a few ideas:

♡ Make a family tree from a tree branch and attach pictures of your family as ornaments.

♡ Make felt puppets or paper sack creations.

♡ Trace chalk figures on the unfinished wall in the basement (or trace them on large sheets of paper), and date them.

♡ Fill a vase full of different kinds of flowers, with each flower representing a different person in your family.

Use your imagination and have some fun!

10. Create a sense of honor.

Reinforce with your children that it is an honor to belong to your family. Tell your children often what an honor it is to have each one of them in your home and how very much you love being a family together. Family prayer is one of the best times to let your family know how you feel.

S U M M A R Y

Creating a family situation where each member feels unique, feels a sense of unity, and feels that it is an honor to be a part of the group, will foster greater love between family members. Children will be more dedicated to family values and confident about their place in "the plan." Your family is an important part of your neighborhood, your ward, and your community. Encourage the feeling that you are a team, that obstacles can be met together, that they will always have someone who believes in them, someone to lean on, and those who depend on them to be there in both bad times and good.

8
SHARE
COMMON VALUES

*"For where your treasure is, there
will your heart be also."*

3 Nephi 13:21

Share Common Values

1. Prayerfully consider the values to focus on in your home.

Heavenly Father will inspire you as you prayerfully consider the needs of your family. He will help you determine the values that are most pertinent at a particular time for your particular circumstances. Ask in prayer that *you* may be a good example of these values in your home.

2. Consider these family values as you teach your family.

Review these words and definitions from the dictionary and discuss the meanings and applications with your family.

Love: A strong affection, warm attachment, or unselfish loyal and benevolent concern for others. To cherish, to feel tenderness, devotion, or to take pleasure in.

Loyalty: The quality of faithfulness, especially to a cause, ideal, or each other.

Respect: High regard or esteem.

Gratitude: Thankfulness; a recognition of blessings.

Truth: Actuality. A body of real events or facts. Reality.

Reverence: Honor or respect felt or shown. A gesture of regard, respect, devotion.

Contentment: Ease of mind; satisfaction.

Devotion: The fact or state of being ardently dedicated and loyal (as to an idea or person).

Optimism: An inclination to anticipate the best possible outcome of actions or events.

Unity: The quality or state of being or being made one; oneness, accord, harmony. Continuity without change of purpose. Totality of related parts. Solidarity; union; integrity.

3. Study the Articles of Faith together as a family.

Point out the values contained in each Article of Faith so your family has a clear understanding of what you believe.

4. Involve your children in selecting values and making rules associated with your family values.

You can't just assume that since integrity is an important value, it will automatically be of importance to all members of your family. If you value honesty, emphasize that value with the whole family as you discuss and decide on the rewards or consequences associated with positive or negative choices in that area. Involving family members in making those decisions creates greater "ownership" and interest. "Owning" the value, and the decisions about how to live that value, will help everyone to personalize the values.

As your family decides upon values to live by, and the rewards and consequences associated with those values, use those values as topics for family home evening lessons. Family home evening is a great place to reinforce ideas that come out of your discussion about values and how your family chooses to live them.

5. Display items in your home that serve as reminders of your family values.

A single word in large print on a piece of paper, an object to remind everyone of a story that was told in family home evening, or a photo, quote, or poster can be a visual reminder of a specific value your family is "investing" in.

6. Be engaged with your children in activities that support your family values.

Work teaches responsibility. Service teaches compassion and self-lessness. Don't just leave your children to learn values on their own. Watching you go out the door to work or to serve will not necessarily teach them to value work and service in their own lives. Being together as a family in activities that support your family values will be their greatest teacher.

7. Give your children leadership responsibilities.

Have your children teach a family home evening lesson, call the family to prayer, plan family activities, and so forth. It will be a powerful learning experience and give them confidence to accept leadership responsibilities outside the home.

8. Encourage and support Church-sponsored goal achievement programs.

The Young Women Personal Progress program, the Aaronic Priesthood Duty to God program, the Primary Achievement Days and Gospel in Action Award programs, and the Faith in God Award for Scouts are all worth your family's time and effort. Keep your family involved in things that promote strong characteristics and good moral values. Instill in your children an understanding that their time is valuable, and that it will be a blessing to spend their time in activities that build and strengthen rather than in things that never satisfy.

9. Create a "Treasure Chest of Values."

Since a treasure is a highly prized, precious possession of great worth, discuss with your family what a treasure is, how you would treat a treasure, and what kind of worth it would have. Make your own "treasure chest," and ask a different member of the family each week to place something representing an eternal value inside the chest. These treasures could represent the Savior, prayer, scriptures, your family or each member of the family individually, testimony, unity, charity, service, honesty, revelation, integrity, or anything else your family values.

Examples of objects representing values could be drawings or pictures of someone praying, a set of scriptures, a tithing envelope, or a heart-shaped pillow. Be creative!

10. Create a "garbage can" of things that have no place in your life.

There are certain things that are of no value in any home, things that would be better off buried in a landfill somewhere than getting any time or attention in your own home. These things are in the trash; you can't and don't want to retrieve them. There may be a particular music group that you symbolically throw away, a few television shows that you throw away, or words that you vow not to use in your family. Consider throwing away gossip or finding fault with one another. Take the opportunity to throw away laziness, unkindness, and negative thoughts or negative self-talk. Tell your family that once these things are in the trash, you don't want to retrieve them or use them again.

SUMMARY

When a family decides together what they value and works toward a common goal, they give themselves a gift of unity, of oneness in purpose. Agreeing upon what you value makes it easier for your family to see what is important and what will carry you through the storms of life. As you incorporate into your lives the values you have chosen as priorities, you become more like our Savior and less like the natural man we are commanded to "put off." Our families will gain much strength from agreeing on and working toward values together.

9

TEACH PRINCIPLES, NOT JUST RULES

"We believe that the first principles . . .
of the Gospel are: first, Faith in the Lord
Jesus Christ; second, Repentance. . . ."

Fourth Article of Faith

Teach Principles, Not Just Rules

1. Understand the difference between principles and rules.

What is a principle? A principle is a basic truth or law that is eternally correct. It usually has a promise that goes with it.

What is a rule? A rule is a prescribed direction for behavior. Rules help us live the principles we know to be true.

Most people have a tendency to rebel against rules, to feel that they are a restriction, or to question why rules are needed. Although rules are meant as a safety net or a protection, if the *principles* behind the rules are not explained, *rules* can be seen as an infringement of or a limit to freedom. A wisely taught principle, on the other hand, makes sense out of the need for rules to govern behavior.

Principles have an eternal connection. Perhaps that is why we have been asked to teach the principles of the gospel in our families. When we live a gospel principle, a fulfilled promise will result.

2. Teach the difference between principles and rules to your family.

Explain the concept by using the principle of jet propulsion. While jet propulsion doesn't have an effect on our eternal life, it can be used as an example of a principle with precise rules to help us understand why both are important.

To achieve jet propulsion, many rules need to be followed. Together, the rules make possible a formula that consists of the right ingredients, in the right amount, and in the right order. When the rules or formula for jet propulsion are applied exactly, a plane can fly. If the rules are not followed exactly, or if they are changed in any way, the plane cannot fly. What you put into it is exactly what you will get out of it. Not following the rules will result in failure and disappointment.

3. Teach the gospel as principles instead of a list of rules.

Students can often recite several of the *rules* that govern conduct in their school: No chewing gum in class, no running in the halls, and so forth. The *principle* behind these rules is respect for others. A licensed driver can name several traffic *rules* for safe driving: Obey the speed limit, stop at a red light, and so forth. The *principle* behind these rules is safety. Many people the world over can list at least some of the Ten Commandments: "Thou shalt not steal," "thou shalt not bear false witness," and so forth. The principles behind these commandments—or rules—is love of God and fellowmen.

The principle of respect at school requires that rules be followed, but respect is about more than rules. The principle of safe driving requires rules but encompasses much more than a list of traffic laws. Similarly, the gospel of Jesus Christ is not just a list of rules or commandments we must obey. As the Primary song "I Am a Child of God" reminds us, the gospel of Jesus Christ encompasses all the principles that our Heavenly Father has given us to understand and live in order to be happy and to live with him again one day.

Living the principles of the gospel is different from just obeying rules. When we truly live the principles of the gospel, we follow the correct "formula" for happiness by using the right ingredients, in the right amounts, and in the right order. What we put into it is exactly what we are going to get out of it.

4. Teach your family how to live based on principles.

As a family, consider why the rules were given. Look at a commandment—and then examine it a little deeper, trying to discover the principle behind the rule. For instance, most Latter-day Saints are familiar with the *don'ts* of the Word of Wisdom: No alcohol, no tobacco, no coffee or tea. (See D&C 89.) But the Word of Wisdom also contains *do's* regarding the use of meat, grains, fruits, and vegetables, in addition to promises of health, strength, and wisdom. What is the principle the Lord is trying to teach us through these "rules"? If we understand that our bodies are precious gifts from a loving Father in Heaven, it is easier to want to obey the "rules" associated with the principle of good health.

Many of us are inclined to obey some commandments or rules and ignore others. Perhaps this is because we don't understand the principles behind the commandments. Sometimes it is easier to "cuddle up" to the commandments that are comfortable for us, living "the letter of the law" while neglecting the principle—or spirit—behind the rules. When we consider *why* a particular rule was given, our families can better understand the purpose in obeying it. This will be a great help in deciding how to live the entire principle. (And you may encounter less rebellion against difficult rules!)

5. Relate gospel principles to daily living.

When your child is confronted with a difficult decision—perhaps the temptation to wear an immodest prom dress, to cheat at school, or to participate in an inappropriate Sunday activity—ask him or her to help you decide what principle is involved and what rules will help them live that principle. Your children will have more ownership of the ultimate decision and will have less of a tendency to rebel as they understand the purpose of the principle.

Principles can remind us of our Heavenly Father's love and his desire to protect us. Discussing gospel principles with your family on a daily basis and teaching the purpose behind gospel principles in family home evening or in Sunday night discussions can help your family relate these principles to their daily lives.

6. Teach the atonement of Jesus Christ as a guiding principle.

Make it perfectly clear to your family: The principle of the Atonement applies to each and every one of us *personally.* Help your family understand that our Savior gave his life for all of us because he loves us and because our Heavenly Father loves us. While we did not, cannot, and will not ever be able to *earn* it in this lifetime, in some amazing way we are worth the price he paid. We can, however, earn a deeper appreciation of that divine love through our faith and obedience.

When your family truly understands the Atonement and the connection between the worth of souls, repentance, and forgiveness (see D&C 18:10–11), it will become a guiding principle that will help you live your lives appropriately. To help teach this principle and how it relates to our daily actions, read the books *Believing Christ* and *Following Christ* by Stephen E. Robinson.

7. Remember the principle of how a testimony is built.

It is a little like building a house. You don't want to throw up drywall and get it painted without first having a strong foundation, sturdy and reinforced, and in the right place. (Remember the first rule of real estate: location, location, location!) The same is true of a testimony—it must be based on a sure foundation. While all of the elements of a house are important, each needs to be added at the proper time and in the proper place. A testimony is built the same way—line upon line, precept upon precept.

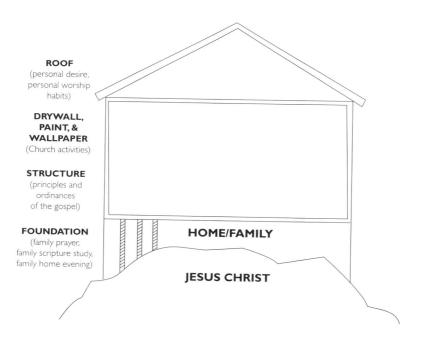

ROOF
(personal desire, personal worship habits)

DRYWALL, PAINT, & WALLPAPER
(Church activities)

STRUCTURE
(principles and ordinances of the gospel)

FOUNDATION
(family prayer, family scripture study, family home evening)

HOME/FAMILY

JESUS CHRIST

8. Teach the principles of spiritual health and well-being.

The principle of spiritual health can be compared to the principle of physical health.

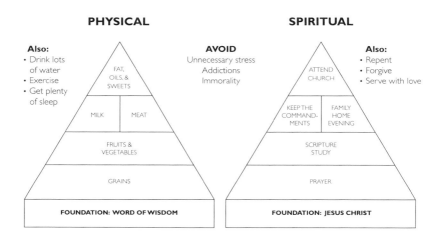

9. Understand the principle of planting and nourishing the seed.

If you were given a choice seedling and wanted it to grow and give you pleasure for many years to come, you would be very careful where you chose to plant it. Hoping to give it both firmly fixed roots and a place in the sky, you would not plant it in rocks where it wouldn't get lots of water and rich soil. You wouldn't deprive it of necessary light and nutrients and count on fertilizer alone to make it grow. You would give your seedling the best possible chance at growth by providing all the necessary ingredients.

Your children are choice seedlings. In order for them to grow in the gospel and develop strong testimonies, they must be given all of the necessary ingredients. Don't count on some spiritual Miracle-Gro shortcut to do it all for you!

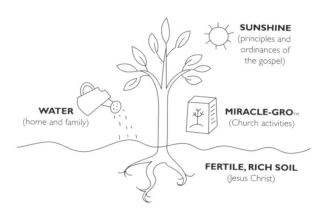

SUNSHINE
(principles and ordinances of the gospel)

WATER
(home and family)

MIRACLE-GRO™
(Church activities)

FERTILE, RICH SOIL
(Jesus Christ)

10. "Teach them correct principles and [let them] govern themselves."

This statement from Joseph Smith (*Millennial Star* 13:339) does not mean that you leave your children alone to fend for themselves. Rather, teach your children correct principles and allow them to help you decide on rules that will obtain the desired results. An example would be to choose the principle you want to discuss, read about it from the scriptures or the Gospel Principles manual, and then ask your family to help you decide what you *can* do and what you *shouldn't* do. To live the principle of modesty, for example (an equal challenge for both girls and boys), the list of *can's* may include being prayerful, being thoughtful, being humble, and so forth. The list of *can'ts,* of things to avoid, would include competitiveness, aggressiveness, comparisons, loud speech, extravagant or skimpy dress, and so on. Always start with the list of *can'ts*—it will help you put the principle in its proper perspective. You and your family will see the Father's love in the principle, and his reason for making that requirement. In this case, being modest will strengthen our humility, a key element in strengthening our relationship with him.

Some eternal principles to keep in mind as you set rules to more fully live the gospel are: tithing, modesty, chastity, obedience, sacrifice, charity, and so forth.

SUMMARY

Perhaps the best example of living a principle-based life is shown in Alma 57. The 2,000 stripling warriors are some of the most amazing young men in history! Alma 57:21 contains the key to what made them so spectacular. Mark it in your scriptures. Pray about it. Ponder it.

These young men did "obey and observe to perform every word of command [every principle] with exactness." Every one of them, exactly. And who taught them? Their mothers! That, of course, can easily include their fathers. Parents *are* the most effective teachers of the principles of the gospel, and the home is the basis of a righteous life. A righteous leader can also be important to success, but only in addition to being taught the gospel at home. The stripling warriors governed themselves in righteousness because they had first been taught righteous principles by loving parents in the home. Notice— the scriptures do not say they were perfect. There is a difference between exactness and perfection. While it may not seem possible to be perfect in every way, exactness is a very achievable goal. Remember, what you put *into* it will affect what you get *out* of it.

10
TEACH DOCTRINE—
SHOW LOVE

*"But ye will teach them to walk
in the ways of truth and soberness;
ye will teach them to love one another,
and to serve one another."*

Mosiah 4:15; emphasis added

TEACH DOCTRINE—SHOW LOVE

1. Keep a balance between teaching doctrine and showing love.

Think of *doctrine* and *love* as two sides of a scale. When approaching any teaching moment in your family, strive for an equal balance of each. If you apply these two principles in balance, you need not worry whether or not you are "doing it right"—because you will be.

2. Don't be hesitant to teach doctrine.

You do not have to understand everything about a doctrine to be able to teach its principles and blessings. You don't have to be a scriptural scholar to know that the scriptures are the word of God. You just have to be sincere and invoke the powers of heaven. "Ask, and it shall be given you; seek, and ye shall find; knock, and it shall be opened unto you." (Matt. 7:7.) Understanding doctrine inspires testimony. Learning truth motivates us, and helps us to live what we know.

3. Don't just *feel* love—*show* love!

We think our family knows or understands that we love them. But *feeling* love for our family members is not enough. We need to do even more than *express* love. We need to *demonstrate* love by our actions. Love can be shown through your eyes, your tone of voice, the words or expressions you use, your body language, a smile, a touch, a testimony. Remember that *show* is a verb and connotes action.

4. Plan in advance to both teach doctrine and show love.

When you are asked to give a lesson, prepare a talk, or share an idea in church, you probably think about it, pray about it, ponder it, research it, and rack your brain, calling upon all your creative powers to decide how best to get your point across so that others will understand and benefit from your efforts. Why, then, when it comes to teaching moments with our family—such as family home evenings, Sunday gatherings, or big events such as baptisms, priesthood ordinations, or temple and mission preparations—do we sometimes fall short of putting the necessary time, thought, and effort into teaching them and providing them with an understanding?

In teaching doctrine and showing love we need to put forth an effort. Put some thought into it. You most likely wouldn't stand up in front of the congregation and just read the scriptures word for word. You certainly wouldn't say to them, "I didn't prepare—let's just go bowling!" Don't do it with your family either.

5. Keep both doctrine and love in mind during spontaneous teaching moments.

You can keep the balance of doctrine and love in mind as you encounter those moments with your children in everyday life.

- ♡ Give them a kiss as they get out of the car to go to school, express gratitude for their efforts, and remind them to "choose the right!"

- ♡ Put your arms around them as you walk into church together, and let them know that you love the opportunity to attend together and partake of the sacrament.

♥ Express how much you love the temple each time you go, give your children a hug as you leave, and tell them you'll be thinking of them as part of your eternal family while you are there.

6. Teach your family the doctrines of the gospel in an atmosphere of love, warmth, happiness, and fun.

Family home evening is the greatest place to exercise this principle. Take full advantage of the opportunity to teach doctrine and show love in this setting. There are great ways to teach your family the gospel through games and activities in a spirit of love. Let your teaching reflect the great peace, joy, and happiness that the gospel brings.

7. Teach doctrine and show love as you discipline.

Discipline is a somewhat misunderstood word. It means "to teach" rather than "to punish." Consider the root word "disciple," which means one who accepts and helps to spread the teachings of another as well as meaning one who follows.

Discipline belongs in all families. We discipline our children to help them avoid danger, disrespect, or disobedience. We discipline ourselves to "[put] off the natural man." (See Mosiah 3:19.) Teaching doctrine and showing love has great application with the concept of discipline. Doctrine and Covenants 121:41, 43–44 states: "No power or influence can or ought to be maintained . . . only by persuasion, by long-suffering, by gentleness and meekness, and by love unfeigned. . . . Reproving betimes [at the moment] with sharpness, *when moved upon by the Holy Ghost;* and then showing forth afterwards an increase of love toward him whom thou hast reproved, lest he esteem thee to be his enemy; that he may know that thy faithfulness is stronger than the cords of death." (Emphasis added.) Discipline, then, involves both teaching and showing love. President Hinckley calls it "the discipline of love." (*Ensign*, June 1985, 3.)

There isn't a more powerful teacher than love. Brigham Young said, "Bring up your children in the love . . . of the Lord; study their dispositions and their temperaments, and deal with them accordingly, never allowing yourself to correct them in the heat of passion; teach them to love you rather than to fear you." (*Discourses of Brigham Young*, 1954, 207.)

8. Answer questions with both doctrine and love.

When a child of any age has questions or concerns, point them to a doctrine of the gospel in a spirit of love. When anger enters in, both hearts shut out the other. Our loving Heavenly Father teaches sound principles and gives lots of love. Likewise, we should answer their questions with a balance of doctrine and love.

9. Keep doctrine and love in balance in your own personal life.

To truly live the gospel requires a knowledge of what principles you are to live and how you are to live them. A virtuous life filled with honesty, integrity, and benevolence also includes love for one's fellowmen and love for the Savior. Live a life full of the goodness of the gospel, administered in love.

10. Consider doctrine and love as the two most important ingredients in your family's "shield of faith."

President Boyd K. Packer, in a conference address in April 1995, said: "The shield of faith is to be made and fitted in the family. . . .

The plan designed by the Father contemplates that man and woman, husband and wife, working together, fit each child individually with a shield of faith made to buckle on so firmly that it can neither be pulled off nor penetrated by those fiery darts." (*Ensign,* May 1995, 8.) In considering the shield of faith that you fashion for your family members, remember that it takes both doctrine and love to fashion it, fit it, and design it so that it can withstand the attacks which will surely be launched against it over the course of a lifetime on earth.

SUMMARY

In a 1998 regional priesthood leadership meeting (Salt Lake City, August 1998), Elder Dallin H. Oaks instructed parents on how to be more effective in teaching the gospel in the home. Speaking of the importance of a balance between teaching doctrine and showing love, he gave us a recipe or formula for strengthening our families. His inspired words can be a guide in our efforts to teach and rear and guide our families. If we follow his formula and (1) teach doctrine and (2) show love to our children, then we will be able to strengthen any of our family relationships, but especially the special relationship between parent and child. The scriptures also teach us that our two greatest responsibilities as parents are to teach and to love. (See Topical Guide, "Family, Responsibility to.")

11
GIVE YOUR FAMILY TLC+C:
TIME, LOVE, COMMITMENT, AND COMMUNICATION

*"We must work at our responsibility
as parents as if everything in life
counted on it, because in fact,
everything in life does count on it."*

President Gordon B. Hinckley
(*Ensign*, November 2002, 100)

GIVE YOUR FAMILY TLC+C:
TIME, LOVE, COMMITMENT, AND COMMUNICATION

Give your family your *Time*.

In President Hinckley's book *Standing for Something,* he put to rest the age-old debate concerning which is more important—quantity time or quality time. He says, as a prophet of God, that a healthy dose of *each* is required. The key to remember with family time, then, is quality *and* quantity. Remember the slogan "Family: It's about time!"

1. Put your family first.

2. Have a family night at least once a week. Start it early, end it late!

3. Take your spouse and your children on dates, individually.

4. Eat at least one meal together each day.

5. Take advantage of opportunities to talk to your children. Use the time spent driving them to school or helping them with their homework to find out what's going on in their lives.

6. Attend events that matter to your children. Whether it's music or dance lessons, recitals or concerts, games or athletic events, support your children in the activities that matter to them.

7. Share the household chores. Do them together!

8. Keep the TV off. It is a big hole that time gets lost in. Also limit time spent on computers, electronic games, or other "babysitters." Get your family involved in running errands, working together, or making dinner.

9. Plan specific times for "field trips." Plan family vacations, and especially camping—even indoors in the winter—together.

10. Choose some things you all like to do together. Make it a hobby or other favorite pastime—a reading hour, scrapbooks, music, sports, and so forth.

Give your family your *Love*.

Love is what life is all about! The key is to show unconditional love.

Here are some very simple ways to give your family more love:

1. Express it! Say it! Words are a powerful form of expression.

2. Hug. There is great warmth and security in a hug.

3. Listen. Be quiet, and just listen. Listening says, "I value what you think and feel."

4. Teach. Don't leave this important task for someone else to do, or think it happens by chance.

5. Write notes and letters. Put it in writing. Make your feelings tangible, and express your love in a form that can be reread and cherished.

6. Laugh (but not at others' expense). A little humor goes a long way!

7. Be there and be a safe place. Always be available, in good times or bad, showing you care. Let your children know you won't hurt them in any way and that they are safe with you.

8. Spend time. Spend time *for* them, but mainly spend time *with* them!

9. Be thoughtful and purposeful when giving gifts. The gift is *not* the expression of love. The *giving* is!

10. Serve. Serve your family. Do nice things for them because you love them.

Show your family your *Commitment* to them.

Our families will always do better when we are truly, whole-heartedly committed to doing our very best in their behalf. The key to commitment is desire.

1. Pray for increased commitment.

2. Read inspired literature on the subject of families.

3. Make a list of what you value most in life. God and family should be at the top.

4. Make a list of things you are doing *right* with your family. Give yourself credit for the good things you are doing. Then make a list of things you would like to do better.

5. Decide you have the desire to truly connect with your family. Tell yourself you have the desire!

6. Believe that you are and that you can become what you want to be to your family. Someone once said, "Assume the virtue though you have it not."

7. Be hopeful and realistic about what can happen to your family through your efforts.

8. Make a plan for what you want to accomplish, and stick to it!

9. Get a buddy! Find someone you can answer to about how well your plan is going. It's the same theory as having an exercise partner—you are more likely to walk in the mornings if someone is waiting for you than if you have to do it on your own!

10. Just *do it!* Spencer W. Kimball said it long before it became a well-known sports company motto! "Do it!" Be committed to a happier, more connected family.

Work on *Communication* in your family.

Improve the communication in your family by recognizing that communication is not a skill that is far beyond your reach. The key to communication is sincerity. When you speak sincerely, and listen sincerely, you will communicate well!

1. Listen to understand. Listening is so vital that if you do it well it may be the only communication rule you will ever need.

2. Concentrate on good marriage communication. It won't affect just the marriage relationship—it will impact the entire family.

3. Speak plainly so that others can understand you.

4. Make eye contact when you talk.

5. Think first, then respond.

6. Establish the family as a "safe place" where all opinions are valued.

7. Talk *with* your family, not *at* them.

8. Use labels that show love, that build and encourage self-esteem rather than labels that limit or belittle.

9. Make love and trust a priority.

10. Attack the problem, not the child (or spouse, or parent, etc.). This is another widely recognized rule of communication. The concept is akin to hating the sin and loving the sinner. Separate the behavior from the person. There is a definite line between the two!

S U M M A R Y

TLC usually stands for *Tender Loving Care,* and every family needs good, healthy doses of it on a regular basis. In this chapter, TLC+C stands for four basic ingredients of a successful family life: *Time, Love, Commitment,* and *Communication.* If you keep this four-letter acronym in mind, you will find yourselves better connected as a family.

Ask yourself if one of these simple ideas could help you work through a family problem or cement the bond between you and another member of your family. Your family members will definitely feel valued and loved as you apply these concepts in your relationships with them.

12
Make Family Home Evening a Lifelong Principle

"And thou shalt love the Lord thy God with all thine heart. . . . And thou shalt teach [this] diligently unto thy children, and shalt talk of [it] when thou sittest in thine house, and when thou walkest by the way, and when thou liest down, and when thou risest up."

Deuteronomy 6:5, 7

Make Family Home Evening a Lifelong Principle

1. Devote yourself to the principle of family home evening.

Be motivated and excited, but most important: hold it! Don't make excuses—your children are not too old, too young, too far gone, or too perfect. Don't allow anything else to take priority. Think of family home evening as your opportunity to teach the doctrines of the gospel in a spirit of love in your own family—by word, by deed, by example. Think of family home evening as the number one responsibility in your most important calling—that of parents. Once you are a parent, you are always a parent—family home evening may be a walk in a park with a grandchild or a lunch date with your grown child. It is not just for families with small children or for married couples. Family home evening is a principle with a promise that can bless the lives of your family all the days of your life. As your family grows and leaves the nest, find other opportunities to continue teaching the gospel at occasional gatherings, in family newsletters, or in planned activities.

2. Look at family home evening as a gift, not a burden.

George Durrant said, "Parents who harbor a dream for their children's destiny know that the Lord's family home evening program is like a gift from heaven. It is not something that we *have* to do. It is something that we *get* to do. . . . The prophets have said, 'Children coming from such homes will not go astray.' You can have sons and daughters who are responsible, who desire service, who love virtue, who are strong in testimony, who love and are loved because you have family home evening and share this spirit in your home continually." (*Ensign,* Mar. 1971, 6, 7; emphasis added.)

3. Remember the purposes of family home evening:

♥ To teach the gospel in our own homes and families.

♥ To foster testimony in the hearts of our families.

♥ To bring families closer to our Heavenly Father and his Son Jesus Christ.

♥ To strengthen family relationships and foster love and growth.

For the same reason that the Nephites talked of Christ, rejoiced in Christ, and preached and prophesied of Christ, we hold family home evening today, "that our children may know to what source they may look for a remission of their sins." (2 Ne. 25:26.)

The gospel is true. Teach your family that it is! Don't be afraid to express how you feel. You don't have to be a scriptural scholar to know that it is true. You don't have to be a Gospel Doctrine teacher to understand the blessings of the Atonement. You don't have to understand every passage of scripture to teach one to your children. You can feel confident in sharing your personal testimony.

4. Reserve Monday nights.

This is the one night a week you can have your family all to yourself. Take advantage of it. This is your time! Don't answer the phone. Send the message to your family that nothing is more important than your time together. Don't be guilty of pulling other people from their homes and families for less important things. Avoid Monday night burnout by not overloading your children with too many other activities during the week.

5. Make family home evening fun and interesting.

This is a gospel of *joy!* It is called "the plan of *happiness*" for a reason! Be creative about different ways to teach the gospel.

6. Keep the atmosphere safe, peaceful, and loving.

Family home evening isn't a time to belittle, demean, or put down. Make it an occasion where everyone in the family feels they belong and are important to the success of your time together.

7. Involve everyone in the family.

Each family member should be involved in a successful family home evening. Create as many assignments for the evening as there are members of your family. Take the opportunity to teach as often as possible, but also take advantage of the opportunity to learn from them as well. Without a doubt, some of the best lessons you will have will be taught by your children.

8. Plan and prepare.

Too often we neglect to spend time planning family home evening because we are too busy with other things, such as projects at home, work-related issues, or even Church assignments. Don't our families deserve as much or more of our time as other worthwhile endeavors?

9. Create a family home evening kit.

Plan ahead with topics, themes, and ideas you want to present. Collect all of your teaching tools together in a kit to avoid last-minute panic of "What am I going to do?"

A few items you may want to include are the following:

♡ Scriptures

♡ Family home evening manual

♡ *Gospel Principles* manual

♡ Hymnbook and *Children's Songbook*

♡ Church pamphlets

♡ Gospel Art Picture Kit

♡ *New Era* posters/MormonAds

♡ Church magazines

♡ Paper, pencils, and supplies (include extra game playing pieces)

♡ Family puppets

♡ Footprints or other signs appropriate to family home evening

♡ Lesson planner or calendar

♡ Lists of ideas for lessons, activities, and so forth

♡ Softball or ring toss game

♡ Flannelboard figures

♡ Church videos

♡ Gospel-related games and other games that can be adapted for gospel themes

♡ Gospel-themed books for ideas and activities

♡ Homemade games to reinforce gospel themes

10. Have great refreshments!

Never underestimate the power of food. (Latter-day Saints are famous for always serving refreshments!)

SUMMARY

Family home evening is at the very heart of connecting with your family. The blessings of family home evening extend to every season of life. Consider the words of these latter-day prophets:

Joseph F. Smith and First Presidency: "We advise and urge the inauguration of a 'Home Evening' throughout the Church. . . . If the Saints will obey this counsel, we promise that great blessings will result. Love at home and obedience to parents will increase. Faith will be developed in the hearts of the youth of Israel, and they will gain power to combat the evil influences and temptations which beset them." (*Improvement Era,* June 1915, 733, 734.)

David O. McKay: "We feel to say to you again, with our love and sincere assurances, that the Lord will grant rich blessings to all who will prayerfully and sincerely carry out the [family home evening] program. Our Father will help us as we draw near unto Him and seek to make our homes places of love, and peace, and wholesome, righteous happiness. With our blessings and appreciation, we would say again to parents in Zion: 'No other success can compensate for failure in the home.'" ("To Parents in Zion," *Family Home Evening Manual,* 1966, iii.)

Spencer W. Kimball and First Presidency: "It is with deep concern that we urge you as parents to gather your children around you and build love, loyalty, and companionship in your homes. You are responsible to teach your children to walk uprightly before the Lord. . . . We promise you great blessings if you will follow the Lord's counsel and hold regular family home evenings. We pray constantly that parents in the Church will accept their responsibility to teach and exemplify gospel principles to their children. May God bless you to be diligent in this most important responsibility." (*Family Home Evening Resource Book,* 1983, iv.)

President Gordon B. Hinckley: "We are fearful that this very important program [family home evening] is fading in too many areas. . . . This program was begun back in 1915, 87 years ago. . . . In the increasingly frantic rush of our lives it is so important that fathers and mothers sit down with their children, pray together, instruct them in the ways of the Lord, consider their family problems, and let the children express their talents. . . .

"If there was a need 87 years ago, that need is certainly much greater today. . . .

"We urge, in the strongest terms possible, that fathers and mothers regard most seriously this opportunity and challenge to make Monday evening a time sacred to the family." (*Ensign,* Nov. 2002, 58.)

13
CREATE AND MAINTAIN FAMILY TRADITIONS

"Develop family traditions. Some of the great strengths of families can be found in their own traditions."

Elder James E. Faust
(*Ensign,* May 1983, 40)

CREATE AND MAINTAIN FAMILY TRADITIONS

1. Celebrate birthdays and anniversaries.

Make each birthday and anniversary a special day any way you can. Everyone deserves to be celebrated just because they *are!*

♡ Place the appropriate number of birthday balloons on your child's bed for him or her to wake up to.

♡ Make a trip to the place of the marriage or birth. For an anniversary, perform sealings at the temple.

♡ Honor the birthday child as the "Star of the Week" and celebrate his or her accomplishments in family home evening.

♡ Let the birthday child or spouse choose the dinner menu.

♡ Serve breakfast in bed.

♡ Let the birthday child or spouse enjoy a chore-free day.

♡ Whatever the age of the birthday person, have a birthday party complete with cake, candles, and ice cream.

♡ Write a letter each year to commemorate a birthday or anniversary. Put it in a scrapbook.

♡ Don't *ever* forget these special days!

2. Prepare for baptisms and other spiritual milestones.

- ♡ Teach your child about important ordinances months before the event occurs.

- ♡ Have a "Great Days of Eight" celebration where the one being baptized receives a small gift associated with baptism itself, and a special message each day for eight days leading up to the baptism. If you do not consider baptism as a "gift-giving" occasion, remember to make the day memorable for the child by expressing your love and reinforcing the importance of this very special day.

- ♡ Have a portrait made of each family member as he or she turns eight.

- ♡ Create a display of baptism day photos of your family in your home.

- ♡ Give a set of scriptures, a locket or tie pin, or a photo frame for the event.

- ♡ Use objects to teach about the gift of the Holy Ghost:

    A flashlight and compass to remember that the Holy Ghost will guide them.

    A set of scriptures to remember that the Holy Ghost will teach them.

    A whistle to remember that the Holy Ghost will warn them.

    A blanket to remember that the Holy Ghost will comfort them.

    A framed picture of the Savior to remember that the Holy Ghost will testify to them.

♡ Celebrate this special day in ways they will remember by focusing on the child and his or her choice to do what is right.

♡ Record your testimony in the child's scrapbook or journal.

♡ Participate in the baptism program.

♡ Thank the child for what he or she has brought to your family through righteous choices.

Priesthood ordinations can be just as special. Look for ways to instill a love for and a desire to do all things that Heavenly Father has asked us to do.

3. Give one-on-one time.

It's impossible to overstate how much a child craves one-on-one time with a parent.

♡ Make it a weekly, monthly, or semiannual event, depending on the age of your child.

♡ Do simple things. Extravagance takes away from the time itself.

♡ Never stop doing it. Try to spend one-on-one time with your children even when they are grown and no longer live at home.

♡ Go places they want to go.

♡ Do things they want to do, even if it is playing outer space games or having a tea party.

♡ Hold hands with younger children when you are out together.

♡ Let your child know how much you enjoy the time you spend together.

♡ Keep in mind that the relationship you form will prepare your child for the future. One-on-one time is a great gift that will develop your child's self-esteem.

4. Hold family home evenings.

♡ *Always* reserve Monday night for family home evening.

♡ Hold it more than one night a week if possible.

♡ Hold family home evening monthly for children who are grown and living in their own homes.

♡ Invite grandparents or elderly neighbors once a month.

♡ Get everyone involved in making family home evening successful.

♡ Make a family home evening kit (see chapter 12).

♡ Cherish the time—don't dread it.

♡ Make family home evening something everyone looks forward to with invitations, clues, thoughts, or announcements in advance.

♡ View all teaching moments as extensions of your family home evenings.

♡ Don't miss it!

5. Watch general conference together.

♡ Watch conference together, whether you travel to the church to see it or watch it in the comfort of your own home. Make it a much anticipated, happy time in your family.

♥ Create a tradition of eating Saturday breakfast or Sunday brunch together on conference weekend.

♥ Hold a ladies' night activity during priesthood session with the women in your family.

♥ Have a father-son dinner or ice cream date before or after the Saturday priesthood session.

♥ Do something different. Watch a session in the Conference Center, at your stake center, or outside. Or listen in the car while taking a drive to look at the fall leaves.

♥ For a Saturday session, have "church in your pj's," if possible, complete with pancakes, popcorn, or pizza. Send invitations to these special sessions, in your own special way.

♥ Ask your family to report during Sunday dinner what they learned during conference.

♥ Make a conference bingo game for your younger children. Include on the squares things the children can listen for or watch for. The children can then place a marker or snack on that square when that item is mentioned in conference.

♥ Write a note to your children thanking them for sharing conference with you. In your note, mention something you learned from one of the conference addresses.

♥ Read the conference issue of the *Ensign* the next month as part of your family home evening.

6. Take family camping trips.

Aaahh! No phone, no TV, please! Nothing to do but walk, play games, and hang out together!

♡ Plan a place at least once a year where you can vacation together—completely together.

♡ Have a special place you return to every year.

♡ Try someplace new every year.

♡ Take along thick sleeping bag pads to sleep more soundly.

♡ Camp in the backyard.

♡ Set up the tent and camp in the basement in the winter.

7. Make the most of Valentine's Day.

Love, love, love! Everyone needs to feel loved. Enjoy this fun holiday and the chance to say "I love you!"

♡ Make pink, heart-shaped pancakes.

♡ Use only the colors pink, red, and white for lunch.

♡ Plaster hearts or love notes on your child's bedroom wall or in their locker or backpack.

♡ Cover a bed with Hershey Hugs and Kisses chocolate candies.

♡ Wear red, pink, or heart-covered pajamas.

♡ Send a singing telegram—starring *you!*

♡ Deliver a flower or balloon to school or work.

8. Make Easter a Christ-centered holiday.

♡ Keep secular activities away from your Sunday observance.

♡ Tell the story of Christ's resurrection and bear your testimony. Give family members the opportunity to do the same.

♡ Make and display a basket of plastic Easter eggs on which are written the gifts of the Atonement (resurrection, compassion, forgiveness, salvation, exaltation, and so forth). You may also want to include gifts given by you to him because of your testimony of the Atonement (choose the right, keep covenants, have faith, feast on his words, and so forth.)

♡ Record your testimony for your children's scrapbooks or journals.

♡ Have a traditional meal from the time of Christ that includes fish and honeycomb (a roll spread with honey will do).

♡ Commemorate new life with a new outfit for your child to wear to church.

♡ Place an empty plastic Easter egg in every basket to remind your family that the best gift of Easter was the empty tomb.

♡ Give a gift of religious significance, such as a new CTR ring, a bookmark, scripture marking pencils, a storybook or puzzle of the Savior.

♡ Place the words "We Believe" or "He Is Risen" in your home, along with a picture of the Savior.

9. Keep Christ in Christmas.

♡ Decorate a tree using messages from the Savior's life and atonement as the theme—hope, peace, joy, and so forth. (Sounds like Christmas, doesn't it?)

♡ Send a *family* Christmas card.

♡ Make preparations for Christmas before Thanksgiving so that Christmas isn't a stressful time.

♡ Don't allow Santa Claus to be equal to or more important than the Savior. Santa has a place in our celebration of Christmas, but the main focus should *always* be on Christ.

♡ Display nativity scenes or statues of the Savior as part of your Christmas decorations.

♡ Help your children give meaningful gifts to each other and to their parents. Emphasize the giving rather than the gifts.

♡ Plan a "Sub for Santa" or other major family service project at Christmastime.

♡ Enjoy the music of Christmas, the lights, and the feeling. Keep it a magical time to be a family and to celebrate!

10. Celebrate every day.

Make it a tradition to celebrate just "being":

♡ Look for shapes in the clouds.

♡ Stop and smell the roses (or other flowers).

♡ Hunt for butterflies.

♡ Go for walks.

♡ Read good books.

♡ Lie in the shade of a tree in your backyard.

♡ Watch a bird, a squirrel, or a caterpillar.

♡ Swing on a swing.

♡ Watch the sun set or rise.

♡ Plant flowers.

♡ Look for four-leaf clovers.

♡ Build a snowman.

All of these things will remind you that God is real. You will see him in all of his wonderful creations as you simplify your life, and just *be!*

SUMMARY

Traditions help create unity and uniqueness in families. There are all kinds of families and all kinds of traditions. Traditions don't have to be extravagant or take a lot of time. Focus on important occasions or milestones. It's worth the time and effort. Give your family things to look forward to, things they know they can count on, and things that build their character as you build your family unity.

It is never too late to start a family tradition! You can begin any time to enjoy the closeness and security this practice brings.

14
FEAST UPON THE WORDS OF CHRIST

"Feast upon the words of Christ;
for behold, the words of Christ will tell
you all things what ye should do."

2 Nephi 32:3

Feast upon the Words of Christ

1. Make scripture reading a family priority.

Make the commitment to read the scriptures daily. Begin your family scripture study with prayer and sing a hymn or Primary song to invite the Spirit to attend and increase your understanding. Determine that you *expect* to receive the answers and blessings you seek by searching the scriptures. President Ezra Taft Benson told us that "individual scripture reading is important, but family scripture reading is *vital.*" (*Come, Listen to a Prophet's Voice,* 1990, 33.) He said that if we would "feast upon the words of Christ," particularly in the Book of Mormon, we would "receive a blessing hitherto unknown." (*Ensign,* May 1986, 78.) He also said: "Any man who will not teach his family to read in the scriptures and do that which he has been commanded to do relative to the Book of Mormon is in as much peril as the men who would not enter the ark in the days of Noah." (Gene R. Cook, *Raising Up a Family to the Lord,* 1993, 30.)

2. Encourage individual scripture study.

Offer study plans or incentives to your children. Provide scripture reading charts to track their progress. Introduce young children to the scripture readers available through Church distribution centers and help them establish a habit of personal scripture study from their earliest years as you read these stories together.

Parents need to set the example by studying the scriptures themselves. Study where your children can see you. Share with them insights you gain and tell them of your love of the word of the Lord.

3. Provide each family member with his or her own set of scriptures.

Consider a family tradition of presenting your children with a set of scriptures when they are baptized. You may also consider purchasing a new set when they start seminary. Encourage your children to mark their scriptures during personal and family scripture study.

4. Study, rather than read, the scriptures.

When you read an entire story at a time instead of just a few verses, or a chapter, you will find more significance and meaning in the scriptures. When you don't understand a particular scripture, read it over again and at least one scripture before and after it. Reading in context will usually clear up the meaning.

Occasionally study the scriptures topically rather than sequentially. Use the Topical Guide as a resource, selecting subjects that have particular meaning for your family or for an upcoming event. For instance, before a new temple dedication, you might look up scriptures about temples and discuss them as a family. Studying topics such as love, hope, peace, and charity can make the scriptures seem more personally relevant to your children as you discuss how they might be applied on a daily basis.

5. Use the seminary Scripture Mastery verses in family scripture study.

Obtain a list of the Scripture Mastery verses used in seminary and discuss them as a family. Have family members mark each passage in their individual set of scriptures. Work together as a family to memorize the Scripture Mastery verses or other passages that have special significance to your family. Find occasions, such as a long car trip, to review the scriptures you have memorized.

6. Use the scriptures in family home evening lessons.

Show your children that you really *use* the scriptures by reading directly from the standard works. Ask family members to bring their personal scriptures to family home evening and read along with you. Show during the lesson how the scriptures answer questions or give us "food for thought."

7. Find ways to make the scriptures come alive for your family.

♡ The scriptures are full of object lessons, allegories, analogies, and parables. Create visual reminders of them in your home.

♡ Place scripture quotes on brightly colored papers around the house—on the refrigerator, a mirror, a headboard—or in the family newsletter as a thought to remember or to strengthen your children in a time of need.

♡ Tuck a little piece of paper with a favorite scripture into a lunch sack or a pocket.

♡ Use scripture flannel board figures or pictures for younger children or grandchildren.

8. Discuss with your family the discoveries you make in the scriptures.

Tell how you have found answers to your problems, how the scriptures have increased your understanding, or how you have witnessed the truthfulness of what you believe from your study of the scriptures.

9. Liken the scriptures to our day.

As we "liken all scriptures unto us" we will see that the scriptures are "for our profit and learning." (See 1 Ne. 19:23.) The events and occurrences recorded in the scriptures are similar to the events of our day. We can learn to recognize the warning signs and can receive the promised blessings as we study the lives of those who have gone before us.

10. Develop your own testimony of scriptures relating to home and family life.

You may find special meaning in the following scriptures:

♡ Deuteronomy 6:5–7   ♡ Mosiah 1:1–8

♡ Joshua 24:15   ♡ 3 Nephi 22:13

♡ Malachi 4:5–6   ♡ D&C 25:26–28

♡ 3 John 1:4   ♡ D&C 88:119

♡ 1 Nephi 8:10–16   ♡ D&C 93:40, 50

♡ 2 Nephi 25:26–27   ♡ Moses 6:56–58

SUMMARY

Reading the scriptures is not like reading a novel; the people of the scriptures were real, with real stories to tell. Their voices call out to us and we can learn from their lives and their choices. The words recorded in the scriptures are there for specific reasons and we can be assured that they are the words of Christ. The scriptures can help us build and strengthen our families on a daily basis. As we make a greater effort in our families to read, to understand, to learn, and to live what we read in the scriptures, we will be blessed in all areas of our lives. We will find greater ability to resist temptation for us and our children. We will all draw nearer to our Father in Heaven.

15
FOLLOW THE
PROPHETS

*"All those from the beginning, . . . who
believed in the words of the holy prophets,
who spake as they were inspired by the gift of
the Holy Ghost, who truly testified of him in
all things, should have eternal life."*

Doctrine and Covenants 20:26

Follow the Prophets

1. Express gratitude for the prophet in your family prayers.

Pray for the prophet's health, his strength, his energy. Give thanks for the guidance brought to your life and express that you know he speaks for Heavenly Father, and that you know he does so in love.

2. Follow the words of the prophets in your own life.

Never dismiss the prophet's counsel. Talk to your children about how you are trying to follow the words of the prophets in your own life. No matter how old your children are, your example and your testimony will be of great significance to them.

3. Encourage your children to pray about the reality and divinity of modern-day prophets.

Especially encourage your children to pray for a knowledge that Joseph Smith really saw what he said he saw, that he truly was a prophet. Also, encourage them to pray about the current prophet, and to pray *for* him. They will have a greater ability to sustain him and follow his counsel when they know for themselves that he speaks for God.

4. As a family, learn to recognize each modern-day prophet.

Place a picture of each latter-day prophet in your home, along with a quote from each one. Full packets are available from Church distribution centers at a very reasonable price. Rotate the pictures so that your family will get to know and love each one.

5. Learn Primary songs about prophets.

The song, "Latter-day Prophets" (*Children's Songbook,* 134), teaches the names of modern prophets in chronological order. "Follow the Prophet" (*Children's Songbook,* 110) teaches about ancient and modern prophets and the great wisdom that comes from following their teachings.

6. Get a matching game of the prophets for your family to play.

These games are available commercially, but they are also very easy to make yourself. This can help your children identify the prophets and have an image in their mind of who they are when they hear something about their lives.

7. Study the lives of the prophets.

Study the latter-day prophets one at a time during family home evening. You may want to assign each member of the family to find out everything he or she can about a specific prophet in twenty or thirty minutes, and then report to everyone what was learned.

8. Tell your family what you remember about each prophet.

Talk about how old you were when each man was the prophet and what you remember about him. Discuss who was prophet at the time you were born, baptized, or married. Tell your children who was president of the Church when they were born.

9. Make a family scrapbook to collect things you learn about the prophets.

This is a great home evening activity and provides a good place to keep all of the pictures and activities about the prophets. The Church magazines often have interesting articles on the prophets that you can collect in your scrapbook.

10. Watch general conference with your family.

Ask your children questions about what they learned from the prophet's talk. Raise your hand to sustain the prophet each time you have the opportunity.

SUMMARY

Teach your family what it means to have a living prophet of God on the earth today who tells us what God wants us to know, and who cannot lead us astray. Teach them about the lives of these great men, their testimonies, and the instructions they have labored so diligently to give us.

Joseph Smith: "I saw a pillar of light exactly over my head, above the brightness of the sun, which descended gradually until it fell upon me. . . . When the light rested upon me I saw two Personages, whose brightness and glory defy all description, standing above me in the air. One of them spake unto me, calling me by name and said, pointing to the other—*This is My Beloved Son. Hear Him!*" (Joseph Smith–History 1:16–17.)

Brigham Young: "It matters not whether you or I feel like praying, when the time comes to pray, pray. If we do not feel like it, we should pray till we do." (*Discourses of Brigham Young,* 1954, 44.)

"I care nothing about my character in this world. I do not care what men say about me; I want my character to stand fair in the eyes of my Heavenly Father." (Brigham Young Office Minutes, 24 April 1859.)

John Taylor: "We are not alone! God is with us, and He will continue with us from this time henceforth and forever!" (*Life of John Taylor,* 1963, 325.)

"We say we are the children of God. That is true, we are. We are sparks struck from the blaze of His eternal fire. But what of the rest of the world—whose children are they? They are also the children of our Heavenly Father, and He is interested in their welfare as He is in ours." (*Life of John Taylor,* 1963, 421.)

Wilford Woodruff: "We are expecting to live together forever after death. I think we all as parents and children ought to take all the pains we can to make each other happy as long as we live that we may have nothing to regret." (*Encyclopedia of Mormonism,* 1992, 1592.)

Lorenzo Snow: "Jesus has commanded us to be perfect even as God, the Father, is perfect. It is our duty to try to be perfect, and it is our duty to improve each day, and look upon our course last week and do better this week; do things better today than we did them yesterday, and go on and on from one degree of righteousness to another." (Conference Report, Apr. 1898, 13.)

Joseph F. Smith: "I feel to say before this people, and would be pleased to have the privilege of saying it before the whole world, that God has revealed unto me that Jesus is the Christ, the Son of the living God, the Redeemer of the world. . . . I know, as I live, that this is true, and I bear testimony to its truth. . . . I know that this is the kingdom of God, and that God is at the helm. He presides over his people. He presides over the president of this Church, and has done so from the Prophet Joseph . . . and He will continue to preside over the leaders of this Church until the winding-up scene." (*Gospel Doctrine*, 1939, 501–2.)

Heber J. Grant: "I know as well as I know anything in this life that Jesus Christ is in very deed the Savior of Mankind, and that God has seen fit to establish the Church of Jesus Christ upon the earth. I thank the Lord that I have pleasure in bearing witness to all the world of this knowledge that I possess." (Conference Report, Oct. 1944, 10–11.)

George Albert Smith: "My grandfather used to say to his family, 'There is a line of demarkation, well defined, between the Lord's territory and the devil's. If you will stay on the Lord's side of the line you will be under his influence and will have no desire to do wrong; but if you cross to the devil's side of the line one inch, you are in the tempter's power, and if he is successful, you will not be able to think or even reason properly, because you will have lost the spirit of the Lord.'" (*Sharing the Gospel with Others*, 1948, 42–43.)

David O. McKay: "God bless us that we may go home with a firmer resolve than we have ever had before to live the gospel of Jesus Christ, to be kind to our families and to our neighbors, to be honest in all our dealings so that men seeing our good works may be led to glorify our Father in heaven. . . . May God bless you all, and may he guide and help you that righteousness, harmony, and love for one another may dwell in each home, I pray." (Conference Report, Oct. 1966, 137–38.)

Joseph Fielding Smith: "If this church were the work of man, it would fail, but it is the work of the Lord, and he does not fail. . . . If we keep the commandments and are valiant in the testimony of Jesus, the Lord will guide and direct us and his church in the paths of righteousness." (Conference Report, April 1970, 113.)

Harold B. Lee: "I know with all my soul that these sayings are true, and as a special witness I want you to know from the bottom of my heart that there is no shadow of doubt as to the genuineness of the work of the Lord in which we are engaged, the only name under heaven by which mankind can be saved." (*Ensign,* Jan. 1973, 134.)

Spencer W. Kimball: "Put your shoulders to the wheel, lengthen your stride, heighten your reach, increase your devotion." (*Teachings of Spencer W. Kimball,* 1982, 564.)

"The Lord will not translate one's good hopes and desires and intentions into works. Each of us must do that for himself." (*The Miracle of Forgiveness,* 1969, 8.)

Ezra Taft Benson: "I would particularly urge you to read again and again the Book of Mormon and ponder and apply its teachings. The Book of Mormon was referred to by the Prophet Joseph Smith as 'the most correct of any book on earth, and the keystone of our religion.' . . . The Book of Mormon will change your life. It will fortify you against the evils of our day. It will bring a spirituality into your life that no other book will. It will be the most important book you will read in preparation for a mission and for life." (*Ensign,* May 1986, 43.)

Howard W. Hunter: "Let us follow the Son of God in all ways and in all walks of life. Let us make him our exemplar and our guide. We should at every opportunity ask ourselves, 'What would Jesus do?' and then be more courageous to act upon the answer. We must follow Christ, in the best sense of that word. We must be about his work as he was about his Father's. We should try to be like him even as the Primary children sing, 'Try, try, try!'" (*Ensign,* May 1994, 64.)

Gordon B. Hinckley: "We are now a people of consequence. Our voice is heard when we speak up. We have demonstrated our strength in meeting adversity. Our strength is our faith in the Almighty. No cause under the heavens can stop the work of God. . . . The world may be troubled with wars and rumors of wars, but this cause will go forward." (*Ensign,* Nov. 2001, 6.)

16
KEEP THE SABBATH
DAY HOLY

"The sabbath was made for man,
and not man for the sabbath."

Mark 2:27

Keep the Sabbath Day Holy

1. Remember why the Sabbath day was created.

The Sabbath day is a day to turn our thoughts more directly to the Lord and to worship him. Because he loves us, Heavenly Father created the Sabbath as a day of rejuvenation and renewal. Observing the Sabbath brings the strength and capacity to face the other days of the week. The commandment to "Remember the sabbath day, to keep it holy," found in Exodus 20:8, is a principle that gives back more than is asked. Honoring our Father in Heaven and his Son Jesus Christ on this day will give us the strength and courage we need to carry us through life.

2. Decide as a family how to live the principle of the Sabbath.

Set the day apart from other days. Teach the principle first, and then decide as a family how to live that principle: "We can keep the Sabbath day holy by . . . We will keep the Sabbath day holy by *not* . . ." Teach the Sabbath day as a principle, and allow your family to decide the formula for success together.

3. Focus on what you *can* do on the Sabbath.

If you focus on things you *can* do on the Sabbath day, instead of things you *can't* do, you will find your family has less of a tendency to murmur about this holy day.

4. Use Saturday wisely to prepare for Sunday.

Remember the Primary song, "Saturday." (*Children's Songbook*, 196.) Always consult the *Children's Songbook*. There is a little something of everything-you-ever-really-needed-to-know in there!

5. Set the appropriate tone for a day of rest.

It is difficult to create a Sabbath atmosphere in your home with secular music or television programs blaring in the background. Take the opportunity to focus on religious and inspirational music and programs. Church videos and music from the Mormon Tabernacle Choir will help set the tone.

6. Be an example of reverence.

Reverence is more than just being quiet. It is the attitude with which you approach the Father on his holy day. Your own personal honor of and respect of the Sabbath will be the greatest teacher to your family.

7. Attend church.

Be active in worshiping and in sharing fellowship and friendship with others on this day. Be a participant in class and an active learner. Feel the good spirit that is present when many faithful people gather together to worship the Lord. Never miss an opportunity to partake of the sacrament.

8. Serve in a church calling.

Offer service willingly. Help others gain a testimony of the gospel and strengthen their families through your efforts. It will strengthen yours, too!

9. Spend time with your family.

One of the main purposes for the Church's consolidated meeting schedule was to allow more time for families to be together. Use this time wisely. In a letter from the First Presidency in February 1999, leaders and parents were admonished to limit Sunday meetings outside of the regular block. The purpose? Once again, it was to give families more time together. Don't let other less valuable things like television crowd in and take over.

10. Keep a box of Sunday activities.

Your box of "boredom busters" might include:

- ♡ Family home evening lessons
- ♡ Family history projects
- ♡ Church publications and magazines
- ♡ Gospel games
- ♡ Flannel board and figures
- ♡ Scriptures
- ♡ Journals (to help get the creative juices flowing, provide a jar of questions or statements to write about)
- ♡ "Happy books" (small notebooks or journals in which you write things that make you feel happy)
- ♡ Church videos

- ♡ Stationery for letters to missionaries or other family members (keep the addresses handy, and include stamps and preaddressed envelopes)

- ♡ A hymnbook and *Children's Songbook*

- ♡ Specialty crayons or markers (for Sabbath use only)

- ♡ Duty to God and/or Personal Progress workbook

- ♡ Scout handbook and/or Achievement Days workbook

- ♡ Scrapbook items

- ♡ Other appropriate activities

SUMMARY

When the Lord revealed the Ten Commandments to Moses on Mount Sinai, he gave them in a very specific order. Each of the first four commandments has to do with our relationship to God. We are commanded not to have any other gods before him, not to make graven images to worship, not to take his name in vain, and to remember the Sabbath day to keep it holy. Keeping Heavenly Father's day holy is an important part of honoring him, worshiping him, and showing our love for him. As is often the case, this commandment requires very little when compared to the greatness of the blessings we receive from keeping it. Our families will benefit greatly by having this day of rest to worship, honor, and show love for our Heavenly Father.

17
TEACH THE VALUE OF WORK

*"Thou shalt not be idle; for he that is
idle shall not eat the bread nor wear
the garments of the laborer."*

Doctrine and Covenants 42:42

Teach the Value of Work

1. Teach the value of work as a principle.

Have your children help you decide how this principle will be applied in your family. Perhaps your motto will be "a place for everything and everything in its place." Maybe your family will resolve not to go to bed in a messy room, or to limit TV or video games. You might establish a set of rules to help your family live according to the principles in Doctrine and Covenants 88:119, creating a house of order. You can determine a set of rules for your individual family designed to help you live the principle of work more fully.

2. Work cheerfully while doing any form of work.

Good cheer takes the drudgery out of tasks. You may want to hang up a sign in your home that states, "To be happy, don't do whatever you like—like whatever you do."

Show your children by example how to do that as you work— smile, sing, talk, laugh. Remember what you are trying to teach your family. You want them to feel that their efforts contribute to the overall well-being and productivity of your family. Your goal is not to be known as the world's greatest housekeeper, but to teach the character trait of responsibility that is so often absent in some of the youth and adults of the world today.

3. Work together as a family.

Strive to make work pleasant and, when possible, something that can be done together. Your family will benefit from having individual responsibilities and chores, but consider the benefits of a family working as one, using the time to connect with each other—to talk, to laugh, to simply be together—working toward a common goal.

Think of your family as a team, even if the tasks are somewhat divided. Each member of the team may have a different assignment, but the goal is a common one for all involved.

4. Assign chores to do in the home.

A child of any age level can contribute in the home. Make tasks age-appropriate. Rotate the chores among family members to provide a little variety. Be specific and realistic about the chores that need to be done. Don't expect too much, and keep in mind the load they may already be carrying. Children will appreciate the ability to complete a task in a way that meets your expectations. Be firm but flexible. Remember, it is a rare day when you accomplish your entire list of things to do.

5. Be creative in making assignments.

Add a little variety and fun to the way assignments are given. ·

♡ Write all of the jobs that need to be done on slips of paper and tuck each one inside a different balloon. The children must pop the balloons to get their assignments.

♡ List all of the chores on separate slips of paper and include on each slip a different clue for finding a hidden treasure. Put the slips of paper in a jar for the children to draw from. Each child chooses a different chore and clue, and as they complete the chore, it leads them to a new clue. You can have these clues and chores lead to a single treasure or to different treasures for each child.

♡ Assign a pretend dollar amount to each chore well done, and then play a game (such as Monopoly), with each child using the money that he or she earned.

♡ For each completed task, award play money that can be used to purchase movie snacks. Watch a video and set up a snack counter where children can buy snacks with the play money they have earned.

♡ Use real money as an incentive, and treat the family to an evening of bowling or miniature golf with the earnings.

♡ Announce that a surprise inspection of the bedrooms in the house will occur during the week. Whoever has the cleanest room will be excused from Saturday chores.

♡ Toss some spare coins into the messiest room of the house. To retrieve a coin, the item it is touching or nearest to must be put away.

6. Resist the temptation to do the work yourself.

Yes, you probably are more efficient and can probably do it better, but what benefit are you giving to your children if you do all the work? Discipline and responsibility are learned as children are taught the value of work. This cannot be done merely by sending your child off to do a job alone, or by your children watching you do a job by yourself. Training is an important key to getting the result you want.

7. Focus on the rewards of work.

Give careful, prayerful, conscious thought to your system of rewards and punishments with regard to work. It is unrealistic to insist that a child work for *every* privilege. On the other hand, giving a child every privilege without any work is not the answer either. Not all work should be associated with earning money or spending time with friends. Give thought to the individual needs of each child and strive for a consistent balance. Punishing with work or punishing because the work isn't done to your satisfaction may lead to resentment. Focus instead on the rewards of work. Work completed, work well done, work done with a cheerful attitude and without being reminded—all deserve rewards. Let your child know that your love will never be withdrawn because they make mistakes. Your system of rewards and punishments for work will speak volumes about your objectives and your unconditional love.

8. Teach your children to care for their surroundings and possessions.

The prophets have admonished us to care for our homes and their surroundings, to plant gardens, and to keep things well-maintained. (See Spencer W. Kimball, *Ensign*, May 1976, 124–25.) Take appropriate and careful pride in the condition of your home. This isn't the kind of pride that says, "We're better than other people." It isn't the kind of pride that leads you to live beyond your means or teaches your family to try to outdo someone else. This is the kind of pride that says, "We're grateful for what we have, and we will care for it appropriately." Teach your children gratitude as you care for what you have.

9. Teach children to be consistent with their personal responsibilities.

Tasks done in behalf of the whole family are usually called "chores." There are also certain personal tasks that need to happen every day, such as hygiene (especially brushing teeth), making the bed, picking up clothes, practicing a musical instrument, homework, and so forth. Perhaps you could call these tasks "personal responsibilities." Even prayer could be considered a "personal responsibility," but be careful not to make it sound like a "chore."

10. Say "thank you!"

Your family deserves to feel appreciated for what they do, whether or not it was an assigned task. Be generous in expressing your thanks.

SUMMARY

We live in a world of convenience. We want things fast and we want it to be easy, with as little effort exerted as possible. Work is possibly the most overlooked of the values that can strengthen families.

In "the olden days," families worked side by side on farms. The father, the mother, and the children were all responsible for the productivity and well-being of the family. Work was the main activity of every day.

The ability to work has been a blessing since the beginning of time, as it is to our families today. There is great value in a family working together—and not just for providing relief to over-fatigued mothers. Consider the following definitions from the dictionary as you imagine the good things that can happen as your family develops effective work habits. In education, there are three Rs: Reading, 'Riting, and 'Rithmetic. With work, there are *four* Rs:

Responsibility: The ability to fulfill one's obligations, or to be accountable for one's actions.

Respect: Concern, esteem, or regard for others and their property; lack of interference with their rights.

Resourcefulness: The ability to solve problems, to overcome, to rise up, to meet and handle situations.

Reverence: The act of showing honor, devotion, or regard.

Keep the four Rs of work in mind as the goal for your family as you structure the atmosphere of work in your home.

18
Use Music to
Usher in the Spirit

*"Yea, the song of the righteous is a prayer
unto me, and it shall be answered
with a blessing upon their heads."*

Doctrine and Covenants 25:12

Use Music to Usher in the Spirit

1. Acquire the hymnbook and *Children's Songbook* for your home.

Make sure you have both the hymnbook and the *Children's Songbook* accessible for your family to use often. Recordings of the hymns and Primary songs are also helpful.

2. Participate in singing hymns at church.

Make sure *you* sing during sacrament meeting. Share the hymnbook with your children and teach them how to follow the verses.

3. Sing a gospel song when you gather for family scripture study and family prayer.

Your understanding of the scriptures will increase and your prayers will be more sincere because you have taken a few moments to invite the Spirit into your home through sacred music.

4. Turn the TV off, and turn good music on.

Listen to sacred music in your home on the Sabbath day and even during the hour prior to family home evening. Use sacred music to set the mood in your home on any occasion and not just on Sunday and Monday.

5. Listen to uplifting music while you drive.

Sometimes you need to turn the radio off in your car to be able to communicate as a family, but driving in the car can also be a good time to listen to uplifting music. Take advantage of this time to play music that is soothing to your soul. Classical or soft instrumental music can smooth the rough edges, give your temper a longer fuse, and provide some moments of peace. You can also use this opportunity to introduce your children to music they might not choose for themselves.

6. Use music to teach values.

There is a wide range of wonderful contemporary LDS and Christian music with inspiring lyrics and uplifting themes. Many of these songs are based on gospel values and can be powerful teaching tools. You might want to create a lesson for family home evening using the lyrics of an inspirational song. Copy the words as a handout for your children and have them read along while you play the song. Share how you feel about the words of the song before or after the song is played.

7. Choose music with faith-promoting lyrics.

Choose music with faith-promoting lyrics for casual listening in your home. Both children and adults will benefit from uplifting and inspirational messages. Discuss with your children the impact that immoral or vulgar lyrics can have if they listen to that type of music. Make inspirational music available to your children so they can be influenced by good music instead of what is so prevalent in the world today. You will likely end up enjoying the music, too!

8. Encourage your children to learn to play a musical instrument.

There are many benefits to learning how to read music and play a musical instrument, including the connection between music and better grades. You may wish to take up a musical instrument yourself or make it a family goal. If acquiring one is at all possible, a keyboard or piano will add much to your home.

9. Play family games based on music.

Play "name that tune" or "musical chairs" with gospel music. This is a great way to familiarize children with hymns and Primary songs.

10. Learn new songs. Sing together as a happy way to pass time.

Learn the hymns and songs from the hymnal and the *Children's Songbook*. Also, new music is occasionally included in the Church magazines. Make it a fun family activity to get together and sing. Show your family how much you value music by making it a family pastime.

SUMMARY

Music has the ability to alter our mood or affect our thinking. Most importantly, however, it has the ability to usher the Spirit into our lives and into our homes. Use the power of music to enhance and strengthen your family life.

Choice of music doesn't need to be a point of contention between parents and their teenagers. There are dozens of wonderful choices for you and your family that will welcome the Spirit, familiarize your children with the gospel, or provide Christian-based, faith-promoting music to listen to. As the world of acceptable secular music narrows, you can be assured that there are many religious artists and recordings to turn to as you seek to enhance your family life through music. Enjoy some great music in your home, and enjoy the spirit that good music naturally brings.

The following lists are just a sampling of the many different artists and recordings available for you to use in strengthening your family. They are not necessarily endorsements, but each artist or group has done beautiful Christian-based work for your family to enjoy regardless of the different styles of music you may prefer.

A few favorite picks from LDS recordings and artists:

EFY recordings (created under the direction of BYU's Especially for Youth program)

Favorite seminary recordings

Recordings based on the Book of Mormon, Doctrine and Covenants, and the Old and New Testaments (available through Church distribution centers)

LDS-themed musical productions (such as *Light of the World, Saturday's Warrior, From Cumorah's Hill*)

The Mormon Tabernacle Choir and Orchestra at Temple Square

Groups: Colors, Jericho Road, Ryan Shupe and The Rubber Band

Male songwriters and vocalists: Kenneth Cope, Peter Breinholt, Shane Jackman, Greg Simpson, Doug Walker, Michael Webb

Female songwriters and vocalists: Cherie Call, Julie de Azevedo, Katherine Nelson, Hilary Weeks

Contemporary instrumentalists: Kurt Bestor, Enoch Train, Jon Schmidt, David Tolk

A few favorite picks from contemporary Christian artists:

Groups: 4 Him, Caedmon's Call, DC Talk, Jars of Clay, Newsboys, Third Day

Male songwriters and vocalists: Steven Curtis Chapman, Michael English, Ronnie Freeman, Bebo Norman, Fernando Ortega, Chris Rice, Michael W. Smith

Female songwriters and vocalists: Susan Ashton, Rachael Lampa, Nichole Nordeman, Michelle Tumes

19
LOVE AND HONOR
YOUR ANCESTORS

"Behold, I will send you Elijah the prophet
before the coming of the great and dreadful
day of the Lord: And he shall turn the
heart of the fathers to the children, and the
heart of the children to their fathers."

Malachi 4:5–6

Love and Honor Your Ancestors

1. Display a family group sheet in your home.

Complete a family group sheet of at least four generations and frame it for display in your home. Try to use a picture pedigree chart if possible. You and your children will be reminded of how important your ancestors are to you.

2. Create a family "Hall of Fame."

On a wall of your home, display photos of ancestors to establish your family's great heritage. Call it the "Hall of Fame" to emphasize how important these people are.

3. Display pictures of your ancestors in your children's bedrooms.

Select, or let your child choose, specific ancestors for your family to learn about and emulate. A photograph will help your child identify with that ancestor as they would a well-known friend. As children come to know their stories, and gain from their experiences, your ancestors can become your children's heroes.

4. Make a scrapbook or history book of your ancestors.

This can be the first volume of your family history. Include as many photos as possible, with brief histories for your children to read and look through often.

5. Celebrate birthdays or other important dates in the lives of your ancestors.

Have a party to commemorate important events such as wedding anniversaries, the day an ancestor was baptized, or the day their family came to this country. Learn about an ancestor's trade or occupation and share it with your family on a day that is significant in that ancestor's life.

6. Visit places of importance in the lives of your ancestors.

Take a field trip to a place connected with your ancestors. It may be just around the corner or require you to travel a long distance. Talk about what happened there, the significance of the place in your ancestor's life, and the importance it has in your own life.

7. Involve your entire family in doing temple work with family names.

As soon as children turn twelve, they can do baptisms for the dead. Even younger children can help find family names and be involved in the celebrations that naturally follow such spiritual experiences.

8. Create ancestor games for your family to play.

Place photos of your ancestors on the game pieces of a jumbo checkers game. You might use one color of checkers for one side of the family and the other color of checkers for another side of the family. Or place photographs of women ancestors on one color of game pieces and men ancestors on the other color. Adding the ancestor's name to one side of the checker is another simple way to help make your ancestors more familiar to your family.

Another game involves writing the names of your family on a few half-size Popsicle sticks. Go back at least four generations and include the names of your children's cousins, aunts, and uncles. Ask family members to choose a stick and describe the person whose name appears on it, and, if possible, to include something about the person's life or characteristics. See how many they can guess! It is also fun to place photographs of your family on card games that you already enjoy playing.

9. Learn about the pioneer heritage that all Church members have.

Your personal ancestry doesn't need to tie in to the early pioneers for you to understand and appreciate the nature of their sacrifice. Make their experience part of your own family. One way to do this is to create board games for your family about the pioneers. Make a trail starting from Nauvoo and ending in the Salt Lake Valley. Along the way, include sites and stories about Chimney Rock, Winter Quarters, and the climb over the Rocky Mountains. You can make playing pieces with photos of early Church history heroes, your own ancestors, or even of you and your family. Your children may understand and appreciate the pioneers' sacrifice more as their game pieces follow the trail through Martin's Cove!

10. Appreciate the legacy you have been given and that you will someday pass on.

Take time now to learn about your parents, grandparents, and great-grandparents. Talk to them and interview them about their lives and their memories. Journals can provide a priceless glimpse into the personal thoughts and feelings of your ancestors. As you learn about their histories, avoid any negative thoughts and judgments and focus instead on the positive aspects of their lives. Cultivate relationships with your extended family and then teach your children of the great values and traditions that have been a part of your family's history.

SUMMARY

The spirit of Elijah includes an undeniable feeling of reverence, honor, and respect for those who have gone before you, and a desire to search them out. Perhaps some of these people know you and are aware of the choices you make in this life. You are a part of their eternal family. The promise given by Elijah wasn't just that you would think of your forefathers and perhaps get their temple work done. The promise said that your heart would be turned to them and their hearts would be turned to you. (See Mal. 4:5–6.) As you study and learn about your ancestors, you connect past, present, and future. You can help your children understand the importance of the legacy that will one day be passed from their own lives to future generations.

Heritage and legacy are about more than direct bloodlines. Every member of the Church has received a legacy from Joseph Smith, his unwavering brother Hyrum, and their amazing mother Lucy Mack Smith. Learning about this legacy helps children understand the virtues of obedience, honor, and sacrifice. Share the amazing past with your family and discover treasures that can strengthen the future. Connecting your family in the present with your family in the past will be an enormous benefit in your everyday life.

20

LOVE THE TEMPLE AND PARTICIPATE IN ITS BLESSINGS

"For behold, this is my work and my glory—to bring to pass the immortality and eternal life of man."

Moses 1:39

Love the Temple and Participate in Its Blessings

1. Have an attitude of love for the temple.

Temples are places of great peace and of deeply spiritual purposes. Much of the work that goes on there is concerned with family. Don't just love to *see* the temple; love the *temple*. Yes, the mere sight of a temple is an awesome thing the world over. These buildings are far different from other buildings of the world. The grounds are always beautifully planted and well maintained. At night, an illuminated temple stands as a beacon, a symbolic reminder to come in from the dark into the light. Primary children sing, "I love to see the temple." (*Children's Songbook,* 95.) Temples truly are a thing of beauty—but what is on the inside is far beyond any kind of beauty that humans can fully understand. This is not just because the furnishings inside are so beautiful, but because of the remarkable work that goes on inside the temple.

2. Prepare to attend the temple.

There is no greater connection for a family than the one created in the temples of God. Temples link children to parents and to grandparents throughout the generations, sealing them into God's family. The Lord wants your family to enjoy the blessings of the temple. Take the steps necessary to enter his holy house.

3. Attend the temple often.

President Boyd K. Packer said, "The Lord will bless us as we attend to the sacred ordinance work of the temples. Blessings there will not be limited to our temple service. We will be blessed in all of our affairs." (*The Holy Temple,* 1980, 182.) Attend the temple not only for the blessings you can receive there, but also for the blessings you bring to others through your work there.

4. Study and pray about the blessings of the temple.

Increase your understanding of the sacred nature of the temples by investing time in study and prayer. Study as an individual, and also as a family, especially as your family grows older and your children prepare to attend the temple. *The Glory of the Temple,* by S. Michael Wilcox, and the classic book, *The Holy Temple,* by Boyd K. Packer, are excellent resources. In your family prayer, thank Heavenly Father for the blessings of the temple.

5. Teach temple readiness from the time your children are very small.

Temple preparation begins in youth. Children can look forward to and prepare for temple blessings by living basic principles. Children can learn to pay their tithing, sustain the prophet, obey the Word of Wisdom, and attend church meetings. Remind your family that they are doing things that will enable them to obtain the blessings of the temple.

6. Live "temple-ready" yourself.

God wants to give you the protection, the peace, the blessings that come from serving in his house. Make the effort to live your life in accordance with readiness to attend and participate. The requirements to enter the temple are not meant to be a restriction, but a preparation. Let your children (whatever their age or current situation in life) know why it is important to you to live your life in such a manner.

7. Express your gratitude for the temple and its blessings to your family.

Thank your children for their cooperation at home while you go to the temple. Tell them how much it means to you to have the opportunity to attend the temple and how grateful you are to have temples.

8. Do work for family names whenever possible.

There is nothing like the feeling of knowing that you are a link in the chain from the past to the future and that you have done a service for someone who cannot do it for themselves. The ordinances of the temple are a prerequisite to exaltation. You need those blessings, and those who have gone before you need those blessings.

With the advances and convenience of modern technology, you can do family history research in your own home *with your children,* beginning even when they are small. Then you can encourage your children to begin doing baptisms in the temple when they turn twelve, whether for family names or for others. Teach them that every season of life is the season for temple work.

9. Show reverence and respect for the temple garment.

The temple garment is a tangible reminder of the covenants we make in the temple. Children need to know that you have a reverent feeling for this gift from Heavenly Father. The garment should not be placed on the floor and should be worn as it was intended to be worn—covered by our outer clothing. We should not let it show, or alter it in order to allow us to dress immodestly. Remember that the garment is intended as a protection for us and should be treated with respect.

10. Make a goal for your family to be all together in the temple.

Whether you are performing baptisms for the dead or attending an endowment session, attending the temple together as a family can be one of the sweetest and most memorable ways to connect with your family. Help your family understand the importance of this goal by establishing stepping-stones or mileage markers to chart your progress along the way, such as baptisms, priesthood ordinations, or achievement in Church awards programs. Encourage each other to work toward making your dream a reality. Regardless of the age of your children, this can be one of the most meaningful ways to connect with your family.

SUMMARY

Remember the words of the Prophet Joseph Smith "concerning the work for the dead": "In the resurrection, those who had been worked for would fall at the feet of those who had done their work, kiss their feet, embrace their knees, and manifest the most exquisite gratitude." (*Encyclopedia of Joseph Smith's Teachings,* 1997, 601.) President Boyd K. Packer said, "No work is more of a protection to this Church than temple work and the genealogical research which supports it. No work is more spiritually refining. No work we do gives us more power. No work requires a higher standard of righteousness.

"Our labors in the temple cover us with a shield and a protection, both individually and as a people. . . . Come to the temple—come and claim your blessings. It is a sacred work." (*The Holy Temple,* 1980, 265, 268.)

21
CREATE HAPPINESS
ALONG THE WAY

"Men are, that they might have joy."

2 Nephi 2:25

Create Happiness along the Way

1. Treat others the way you would like to be treated.

♡ Have high hopes and low expectations.

♡ Dwell on the positive instead of the negative.

♡ Support and defend your family members.

♡ Speak positively of your family (adult siblings and in-laws, too!).

♡ Compliment often.

♡ Be accepting of differences. Don't judge.

♡ Be tolerant and patient.

♡ Concentrate on changing your own attitude, not on changing others.

♡ Give people reasons to smile.

♡ Focus on experiencing life rather than managing it.

♡ Think before you respond.

♡ Encourage family members' dreams.

♡ Give credit where credit is due.

♡ Give others your full attention in conversation. Look people in the eyes when you talk to them.

♡ Share the high times and the low times. Offer assistance to work through problems.

♡ Don't put your nose in where it doesn't belong. Remember—your rights end where the other guy's nose begins.

2. Show affection.

Gestures of affection say, "You matter to me." Show others through your words and your actions that you are committed and care about your family.

♡ Show by your facial expression and body language that you enjoy being with your family.

♡ Give a pat on the back or an arm around the shoulder.

♡ Walk hand in hand.

♡ Smile at your family.

♡ Laugh with them.

♡ Use positive nicknames for family members. Make sure these labels show love and build self-esteem.

♡ Refer to family members with positive adjectives. Don't tear down family members in your conversations with others. Take the opportunity to build them up.

♡ A hug or a kiss is simple but effective.

♡ Express love for your family often, to others and to them.

3. Lighten up!

- ♥ Leave work at work.

- ♥ Don't think about your "to do" list.

- ♥ Chat in a relaxed environment.

- ♥ Let the laundry and housework go for an afternoon and spend that time with your children or grandchildren.

- ♥ Enjoy the four seasons of the year with your family. Splash in the puddles in the spring, build sand castles in the summer, jump in the leaves in the fall, and catch snowflakes on your tongue in the winter.

- ♥ Put your feet up and eat a Popsicle.

- ♥ Go for a walk with a family member. (And don't walk too fast!)

- ♥ Breathe deeply.

- ♥ Accentuate the positive in all situations.

- ♥ Let the past go! Leave the "foolish traditions" of your fathers behind, if necessary. Don't repeat the same mistakes. Live the good and let go of the bad.

- ♥ Focus on loving your family, past, present, and future.

4. Don't let *little* stresses become *big* worries.

- ♥ Don't overemphasize extracurricular activities, especially sports.

- ♥ Be a good sport when family members are involved in athletic events. Always be humble in victory, gracious in defeat.

♡ Don't stress over fashion. It will change tomorrow anyway.

♡ Wear seatbelts and require everyone in your car to do the same.

♡ Clean your house in the winter, and play in the summer.

♡ Speak softly, and lose the big stick.

♡ Don't expect perfection (from yourself or your family).

♡ Focus on what you did right today. Do the same for your children.

♡ Don't compare yourself to someone you think "really has it together."

♡ Remind yourself what your children really want—your love, your acceptance, and security. They want to please you and to spend time with you. They want to feel that they make you happy. (Note that there isn't a single material item on the list.)

♡ Don't talk negatively about others in front of your children.

♡ Don't go to bed angry with your spouse or your children.

♡ Don't let your children or spouse go to bed angry with you.

♡ You can't buy happiness, so don't obsess over money.

♡ Enjoy little moments without some measure of work in your hands.

♡ Be involved in your children's lives on a daily basis in order to be aware of symptoms of a major crisis before it explodes.

♡ Listen to understand.

♡ Get over a grudge. Let go of a past problem.

♡ Be a good parent.

♡ Honor your father and mother.

♡ Remember that happiness doesn't have to wait, it can be found *now*.

5. Let *little* things create *big* happiness.

♡ Make a family member's bed for them occasionally.

♡ Tuck a note inside a lunch or a pocket for later retrieval.

♡ Hug your children before they go out the door.

♡ Put a surprise inside a desk, locker, or backpack.

♡ Have a slumber party in your bedroom.

♡ Sneak your child a high-energy snack before a test or athletic event.

♡ Give teenagers a "get out of jail free" card to use when they've made a mistake.

♡ Send "secret admirer" notes to family members.

♡ Celebrate with balloons at the end of a school term or other milestone.

♡ Apologize when you have been grumpy or wrong.

♡ Write thank-you notes to show appreciation for family members' efforts.

♡ Volunteer at your child's or grandchild's school.

♡ Occasionally watch Saturday morning cartoons together—
before the daily chores are done.

♡ Get *in* the sandbox, or the pool, or the snow, or the mud
puddle *with* your child or grandchild. Don't be just a spectator
all the time.

♡ Display your child's artwork. Draw a picture for them.

♡ Forgive.

6. Create family memories.

♡ When possible, take vacations with your family. Sometimes it's
the only way to get time alone with your teenagers.

♡ Turn your home or backyard into a vacation paradise if you
don't have the time or money to get away. Put up a tent, or give
your home a "hotel" name. You're on vacation, so don't answer
the phone or the door.

♡ Take lots of pictures and make scrapbooks.

♡ Take lots of home movies and show them during a family
movie night.

♡ Play board games together.

♡ Create your own power outage. Turn off all the lights and play
flashlight tag, tell stories, cuddle, and talk.

♡ Throw a big party for a family member for no reason at all.

♡ Celebrate birthdays and anniversaries in a big way.

♡ Share workloads—talk as you do the laundry, cook together, build something together.

♡ Try new things together. Learn to ski, knit, or play the piano; or simply learn a new song.

♡ Talk about "old times." Tell your child what they were like as a baby, and ask them if they remember things that happened in your family.

♡ Play "remember when" and encourage family members to remember events in categories such as "Halloween memories," "funny things that happened," or "most embarrassing moments."

7. Enjoy the holidays.

Create family traditions around the holidays for each month of the year, or turn a "non-holiday" into a traditional family holiday. Choose a date that is of significance to your family, and celebrate your "family day" every year. (Chapter 13 on family traditions can help you think of more ideas.)

January: Ring in the New Year *together* with newly determined focus!

February: Send a family valentine to those you love.

March: Make green pancakes or "green eggs and ham" and tell your family how lucky you are to have them in your life.

April: Dye Easter eggs.

May: Celebrate the lives of those who have gone before you. (See chapter 19 on loving and honoring your ancestors.)

June: Plant a tree.

July: Be patriotic—hold a family flag-raising ceremony, participate in a parade, decorate your house in the colors of your country, or memorize your national anthem. Celebrate state and national holidays.

August: Plan, carry out, or attend a family reunion.

September: Celebrate your last taste of summer.

October: Carve (or decorate) pumpkins as a family activity.

November: Make a list of things your family is thankful for.

December: Sing Christmas carols.

And this is just a beginning—there are many, many more possibilities for family fun every season of the year!

8. Do something crazy once in a while.

♡ Go for a "penny hike" with your kids. Flip a penny at each turn to determine which way to go next. It takes a while to get home, but enjoy it!

♡ Let your children paint their own bedrooms.

♡ Sleep under the stars.

♡ Create an art gallery on your driveway with sidewalk chalk.

♡ Make something nice for someone and deliver it anonymously to their doorstep, ring the doorbell, and run.

♡ Eat dessert first.

- ♡ Serve dinner without utensils.
- ♡ Play before you work.
- ♡ Skip.
- ♡ Let someone get ahead of you in line or in traffic.
- ♡ Kick up the leaves when you walk.
- ♡ Sing with the radio in your car.
- ♡ Give a flower to someone you don't know.
- ♡ Don't worry about what someone else thinks of you.

9. Keep a scorecard only of things that make you happy.

Notice when your family members make you happy in little ways, and ignore the things that bother you. Never keep a scorecard of things that didn't go right. Let happiness, not frustration, be the thing that grows. Your family's "bank account" can overflow with little things that make you happy:

- ♡ Freckles
- ♡ Toothless grins
- ♡ Smiles
- ♡ Your child's eyes
- ♡ Giant efforts
- ♡ Dance recitals
- ♡ First-time band concerts

♡ Cuddling

♡ Hearing your child say, "I love you"

♡ The sound of their voices

♡ Their first-date jitters

♡ Hugs

♡ Finding your children on their knees in prayer

♡ Watching them learn something new or overcome an obstacle

♡ The times they were there when you were down

10. Live your religion wholeheartedly.

♡ Love Heavenly Father. Be humble and let him guide your life.

♡ Love your family unconditionally.

♡ Love your neighbor. Watch and care for your fellowmen.

♡ Remember that everyone is a child of God.

♡ Repent and forgive.

♡ Think eternally.

♡ Keep in mind your place, and your family's place, in Heavenly Father's eternal plan.

♡ Pray.

♡ Read the scriptures.

♡ Follow the living prophets.

♥ Hold family home evening.

♥ Teach your family the gospel.

♥ Be a good example—practice what you preach.

♥ Offer cheerful service to others.

♥ Find joy in living the commandments.

♥ Prioritize correctly: Heavenly Father, family, Church service, and so forth.

♥ Share of your substance. Be generous, especially in fast offerings.

♥ Be grateful for what you have.

♥ Share your testimony with others.

SUMMARY

Abraham Lincoln once said that "most people are about as happy as they make up their minds to be." Never underestimate the power of experiencing simple happiness as a great source of strength for your family. There is much in life we take for granted that could contribute so greatly to our sense of happiness and contentment if we chose to let it. While there are true heartaches and sorrows in life, there is also much to be enjoyed, to be loved, to be cherished, and to make us happy.

Focus on experiencing happiness with your family. You may be surprised how simple it can be to experience more joy and less frustration, more contentment and less worry. Sometimes it will require letting go of preconceived notions or expectations, and other times it will simply take acknowledgment that the things that bring you joy were with you all along. True happiness is not as elusive as we sometimes make it out to be. Life is a journey, not a destination. Happiness is much the same. Find ways to create more happiness along the way, and give yourself less to worry about.

22

Develop an
Attitude of
Gratitude

*"And he who receiveth all things with
thankfulness shall be made glorious; and the
things of this earth shall be added unto him,
even an hundred fold, yea, more."*

Doctrine and Covenants 78:19

DEVELOP AN ATTITUDE OF GRATITUDE

1. Recognize and appreciate the value of each family member—and show them that you do.

Recognition is crucial to feeling valued. When you acknowledge the inherent worth and value of each family member, you offer security, self-esteem, and confidence.

2. Say "thank you."

It seems simple, and it is. But remember that "by small and simple things are great things brought to pass" (Alma 37:6). Expressing sincere thanks often can have a powerful impact in your family and help them learn to identify their own blessings.

3. Express specific appreciation.

Say "Thank you *for . . .*" This is different from just saying thank you. Being specific about what you appreciate in your children will let them know what is important to you, will encourage good behavior, and will help them to identify blessings. Some examples are:

♡ "Thank you for coming in when you said you would."

♡ "Thank you for working so hard on your homework."

♡ "Thank you for cleaning up your room."

♡ "Thank you for being patient with me."

The list goes on and on—as do the rewards.

4. Notice the less obvious.

We live in a world that praises the fastest, the strongest, the smartest, the richest, the most beautiful, and the most popular. There are very few "top" positions to go around. There are no trophies for a courageous heart, no ribbons for sincerity, no medals for great effort, no prizes for kindness. Life should be more about *doing our best* than about *being the best*. Go the extra mile to notice a family member who is doing their best, especially in things that don't typically get noticed.

5. Serve the "blue plate special."

Get a blue plate and use it whenever a family member does something that deserves recognition. Serve the child's dinner on the blue plate and explain to the family what that person did that was special. Perhaps a child studied really hard for a test (the test score isn't the point). Perhaps a child was a friend to someone who really needed it, or stood up for his beliefs in a tough situation. Maybe she practiced the piano without being asked or stopped herself from gossiping. The "accomplishments" can be endless, and this special recognition of their efforts is a way to tell your family, "Thank you for being who you are!" (Used by permission of Sandy Greenwood.)

6. Give awards.

Most people go without recognition for the good they do. The idea is not to teach your children that they deserve an award for every good thing they do, but to provide an award for the things that really matter and to reinforce good character traits. Hold your own "awards ceremony," complete with certificates, ribbons, medals, or trophies. You might want to give an award for:

♥ The kind of friend your child has been to others.

♥ Showing unusual dedication or determination, perhaps enduring to the end with a difficult project or goal.

♥ Achievement in following a family motto—a "Stand Your Ground" award for someone who stood up for their beliefs, or a "Come Up Higher" award to a child who took their grades more seriously.

♥ Each family member, just for making you feel happy.

Recognize your children for the things that others may not notice and for things that really matter—love, peacemaking, devotion, dedication, friendship, integrity.

7. Express gratitude as you pray.

Recognize that every good thing is a gift from God. Let your family hear you pray in gratitude for the gifts you have received. Your family will learn to count their blessings as they hear you give thanks for all blessings, both large and small. Remember that life itself is a gift from God. Recognizing his gifts and expressing sincere gratitude for them is a gift we can give to him.

8. Thank Heavenly Father for each family member by name.

When you pray, specifically name each family member and the particular qualities they bring into your home. Your family will feel especially valued when they hear you pray in thankfulness for their lives and for the kind of individuals they are. Hearing you express how grateful you are that you can trust them to choose the right, or that they get along with each other, or that they provide humor, help, love, and joy in your home can have a tremendous effect on how they feel about themselves and their relationship to you.

9. Be grateful for little things.

If we are quick to point out the little things that make such a big difference and for which we are so grateful, our children will learn to do the same. Encourage gratitude for little things, such as the sound of running water in a creek, a soft pillow for your head, the first tulips of spring, suitcases with wheels, ice cream, butterflies. Noticing little things will give us an attitude of gratitude, and we will discover that some of those things aren't so little at all.

10. Create a gratitude journal.

Record in a journal the things that make you happy, the things that you are grateful for. Have a gratitude journal for each member of the family and do your best to write often. Try to identify one thing each day for which you are grateful. In doing so, you may find your focus shifting from wants and desires to gratefulness for life's innumerable blessings.

SUMMARY

Recognizing our blessings and developing an attitude of gratitude can be a strengthening and comforting force for individuals and families.

Feeling validated and appreciated is a missing link in many family relationships. Everyone needs to feel appreciated. Everyone

needs to feel that they make a difference and that who they are contributes to the whole. Learning to appreciate and show gratitude for each other will bless your entire family. Family members will feel worthwhile to the entire unit and will gain self-esteem and confidence in a home where gratitude for all things is identified and expressed.

23

DON'T CONSIDER YOURSELF THE EXCEPTION TO THE RULE

"There is a law, irrevocably decreed in heaven before the foundations of this world, upon which all blessings are predicated— and when we obtain any blessing from God, it is by obedience to that law upon which it is predicated."

Doctrine and Covenants 130:20–21

Don't Consider Yourself the Exception to the Rule

1. Understand that Heavenly Father loves you and wants you back.

The "work and the glory" that Heavenly Father sent his Son to bring to pass is the immortality and eternal life of man. (See Moses 1:39.) Heavenly Father loved you long before the world began, and his desire is to have you return to dwell with him again. He has given you what you need to make your life more comfortable and happier, to help you experience joy, and to bring your entire family back into his presence.

2. Believe that Heavenly Father hears and answers every prayer.

None of us can understand how he can hear *every* prayer uttered by *every* person in *every* language, at any time and in any place. But we know that he does. None of us completely understands our Father's purposes—and each of us has experienced occasions when a prayer seemed to go unanswered for a long and uncomfortable period of time. But we know that his ways are not our ways. Our eyesight is limited; his is not. Our perception is clouded; his is not. Our time frame is temporal; his is eternal. We wonder how he can possibly know us—we are so small, so insignificant, so unworthy—but he does know us, even to the number of hairs on our heads. (See Luke 12:7.) We are not insignificant to him, and not too small for him to notice. He who notices when a sparrow falls notices when we cry. He is mindful of each of his children, as well as the current condition of our families. While our minds are limited, our hearts can think and know and feel—and our hearts testify that he is there. He desires to have your heart open and drawn to him in prayer. He wants you to ask him for guidance, direction, and help with your family. In some miraculous, inconceivable way, he will hear you, and he has answers for you.

3. Remember that you have a family that needs you.

We seem to live in a world that encourages excuses. It is easy to be fooled into believing that we are bound by limitations we cannot control and that we are the exception to the rule. But there is no exception to the rule that a good family is the cure, the solution, the answer, the best possible place to teach and train—and that every person plays a crucial role.

The term *family* has many definitions, and undoubtedly your situation fits one of those descriptions. No role is more crucial than that of parent, so if you are blessed enough to be a parent, live that role to its fullest! But whether you are single, married, with children, or without children, whether you are old or young or whether your children are old or young, whether your role is that of parent, child, sibling, or grandparent, you can be an influence for good. You can have a great impact on the lives of your family. Young, old, remembered, forgotten, for better or for worse, your family needs you to believe deeply and actively in them.

4. Believe that all families can be forever.

Our Savior Jesus Christ paid the price to make all wonderful things possible, and exaltation is the crowning possibility! You have the opportunity to be with your family forever—with your spouse, with your children, with Grandma, with great-uncle Joe—but most importantly with your Father in Heaven and with your Savior Jesus Christ. It is worth whatever we need to do here to ensure a rightful place to enjoy in heaven forever.

Your family has not lost this opportunity until you give up or quit completely. Heavenly Father wants you to have this blessing, and he will not deny his choicest blessings to the pure in heart.

5. Understand that Heavenly Father holds parents responsible for teaching the gospel in their home. (See D&C 68:25.)

Remember that our Father in Heaven knows your situation. He knows that you are an overwhelmed parent, whether married or single, with a huge list of things to do. He knows your children are small or partly grown or out of the home. He knows you have a mortgage to pay and you feel pressured to offer your children every comfort and convenience in life. He knows you are wrapped up in church work, community service, hobbies, or a career. He knows you have worked hard all of your life and now feel old and alone, but still want to make the most of your family connections. He knows your unique circumstances and situation.

He knew all of Joseph Smith's circumstances when he rebuked the Prophet and other Church leaders for not being more concerned with their families. "What I say unto one, I say unto all," the Lord said, "bring up your children in light and truth." (See D&C 93:40–50.) He knows what matters most. He knows what experiences you need in order to return to him. He has asked that you strengthen your family—no hesitations, no exceptions.

6. Recognize that the Church is meant to play a *supporting* role to the home.

President Ezra Taft Benson said, "The home is the rock foundation, the cornerstone of civilization. The church, the school, and even the nation stand helpless before a weak and degraded home. No nation will rise above its homes." (*This Nation Shall Endure,* 1977, 124.)

President Boyd K. Packer also taught, "The ultimate purpose of every teaching, every activity in the Church is that parents and their children are happy at home, sealed in an eternal marriage, and linked to their generations." (*Ensign,* May 1994, 19.) It is clear that the Church is meant to *support* our efforts at home, not *replace* them.

As parents, therefore, it is important to recognize several things:

♡ We must not relinquish our responsibilities to others, however worthy or appropriate. School, government, even church, should not be the *primary* place to learn values.

♡ Studies show that individual worship practices are best learned in the home with a family that prays, reads, studies, and has family home evening together. In the majority of the cases studied, it wasn't a Church leader who changed or molded a child's life—it was the parents.

♡ You must teach, support, and strengthen at home. You can be your child's greatest teacher. You *are* capable. Be the one to teach and train so the Church can be the supporting player.

♡ Family and Church are not an either-or proposition. Attend church together on a regular basis. The sacrament is indispensable and irreplaceable in your life. You simply cannot survive spiritually without it. But "getting the children to church" is not enough. They must be taught at home as well. *Both* are essential to your family's spiritual growth. (See Gene R. Cook, *Raising Up a Family to the Lord,* 1993, 6–7.)

♥ Church activities should not become so numerous that they replace or hinder family activities.

♥ The Lord will certainly bless you for your service in the Church, but if you are neglecting your family, spending too much time on church work, or assuming that he will take care of other matters for you, you need to think again. Your family is still your first and most important calling in the Church and in life. But remember that "family first" does not equal "family exclusive," so still offer your heart-felt service to the Church. As you focus on your family and are prayerful about your priorities, the Lord will guide you in making the right decisions.

♥ Don't rely on a priesthood quorum leader, a seminary instructor, a bishop, a Relief Society president, or a Young Women leader to do for your son or daughter what is required of you to do for them. Certainly you should be grateful for all that they do, and you should sustain and pray for these leaders in their callings, but don't expect them to do your parenting for you.

♥ If you have a struggling child or spouse, get on your knees and evaluate the spiritual atmosphere of your family, your home, and your relationship to the person in question. Prayerfully ask for help to strengthen your family and lead them to the truth. Remember, you are not just *one* possibility for strengthening your family, you are divinely appointed to be the *best* possibility!

7. Believe that Heavenly Father wants to help you strengthen your family.

Through the voice of his prophet, President Harold B. Lee, the Lord told us that "the greatest work you will ever do will be within the walls of your own home." (*Teachings of Harold B. Lee,* 1996, 280.) Your work at home will be the most valuable and the most important of all the good works you will do in your life. Your prayers for your family, your devotion to the gospel and its principles, and your efforts to build and strengthen the testimonies of your family are worthy of your best work. Heavenly Father can help you understand what will work best. He can help you as you study out a subject in your mind. He can help you overcome any obstacle. He wants you to strengthen your family because it is the unit in which you will live eternally, with him. He can help you "train up" your children, whether they are two or 32 or 52, or even while they are teenagers! To paraphrase the words of Moroni, "Have miracles ceased? Only if your faith has!" (See Moro. 7:35–39.)

8. Realize that success within your home and family will bring the greatest joy.

You will not get to the end of your life and say, "I wish I had spent more time at the office." You will not even say, "I wish I had spent more time at the church." You will face your own mortality with thoughts of your family. When interviewed, survivors of terrible calamities repeatedly mentioned how they thought of their families, and how their perspective changed as a result of their experience. Without exception, they valued their families more than before. As a prisoner in Carthage Jail, Joseph Smith wished he could see his wife and family one more time before sealing his testimony with his blood. Your family is what is essential in life. Your family is where you will find your greatest joy.

9. Realize that it is never too early or too late to connect with your family. (As long as you begin now.)

From the day you are married, you have the blessing of belonging to more than one family. You are still a part of the family you came from, you have joined the family you married into, and you look forward with excitement to the family you create. There is much that you can do at each stage of family life and in each family setting to ensure the closeness, the connection, and most of all, the love you desire. Pray for the members of each family you belong to. Be receptive, be open, and be devoted.

10. Make the most of where you are right now—life passes quickly.

Sometimes it seems as if we will never get out of school, never see the end of diapers, or never have a night out without needing a babysitter. But eventually every one of those days happens and we begin to wonder where the time went. Time is going to march on whether or not you value it. When you are a parent, time seems to go by even faster. Don't wish that your children would hurry and grow up. Don't wish that they would *never* grow up. Cherish who and where your family is today, value the time you have, and live without regret, so that time can be your friend instead of your enemy.

SUMMARY

Life can be a challenge, and there is much to ponder and consider. Sometimes it is easier for us to think that certain principles don't apply to us. We may think we are too old, too young, or that we have tried before and we are tired now. We no longer believe in the simplicity of the message. We want quick fixes or an easy way out. It is understandable that we feel that way at times. When we look at what is best for our families, however, we understand that there *are* no exceptions. There *is* a way, and we can begin *now* to help our families. God has not just given us the responsibility, he has given us the ability and the power.

24
LEARN FROM
THE EXPERTS

*"No matter what the form of your family,
from single-parent household to the largest
multi-generation family in your town,
your work at keeping families together is
the job of saving our world."*

Dr. Paul Pearsall
(*The Power of the Family*, 1990, 351)

Learn from the Experts

1. Learn from Lehi.

In 1 Nephi 8, we read about the marvelous vision of the tree of life. Lehi, a prophet of God, "dreamed a dream" (1 Ne. 8:2) in which he was drawn to a tree "whose fruit was desirable to make one happy." (1 Ne. 8:10.) Nephi later revealed that "the tree of life was a representation of the love of God" (1 Ne. 11:25), which was manifest in the coming of Jesus Christ, through whom the gift of eternal life is possible. Lehi states, "As I partook of the fruit thereof it filled my soul with exceedingly great joy." (1 Ne. 8:12.) What could possibly bring us more joy than to accept and internalize the gift of the Savior, the fruit of God's love for us. To feel his Spirit and to have a personal relationship with him is joy, exceedingly great joy.

Lehi continues, "Wherefore, I began to be desirous that my family should partake of it also; for I knew that it was desirable above all other fruit." (1 Ne. 8:12.) Lehi cast his eyes round about in search of his family and brought them to the tree to partake with him. This portion of the dream profoundly teaches us about God's love and the fruit of that love. We know where the source of exceedingly great joy may be found, and it is our responsibility to take our families to that source, that all may partake together as Heavenly Father intended.

2. Learn from Lucy Mack Smith.

The Prophet's mother was an expert parent. Before Joseph was born, Lucy had a brush with death. She prayed fervently that God would spare her life, that she could be a blessing as a daughter, wife, and mother. She believed that "God kept a warm, personal interest in His children and would hear and answer their prayers." She recorded an experience she had during a serious illness: "The Lord will let me live, if I am faithful to the promise which I made to Him, to be a comfort to my mother, my husband and my children. I continued to gain strength until I became quite well as to my bodily health; but my mind was considerably disquieted. It was wholly occupied on the subject of religion. As soon as I was able, I made all diligence in endeavoring to find some one who was capable of instructing me more perfectly in the way of life and salvation." (*History of Joseph Smith by His Mother,* 1901, 42.)

Little did Lucy know she would give birth to that "some one" whose life would touch all of ours so deeply on "the subject of religion." Lucy was the one who instilled in the hearts of her children the desire to know the truth. It was Lucy who taught prayer and scripture reading to her children as they gathered around the hearth every morning and night. Joseph's belief in God did not happen by chance. The seeds were planted by his mother to look to his Heavenly Father, through scriptures and through prayer, for answers to his questions. Joseph had been taught that God lives and would answer his prayers.

3. Explore the Proclamation on the Family.

Understanding our Father's plan for his children and his divine plan for families will aid you in your quest for family happiness. Take the time to read the proclamation prayerfully, several times. Consider that perhaps the most important question to ponder is why the proclamation was given. The First Presidency's presenting this declaration to the world clearly shows that the subject is of great importance to our happiness and central to the concerns and interests of our Heavenly Father.

Read it again, with fresh eyes, and notice the following points:

- ♥ "The family is ordained of God."

- ♥ "The family is central to the Creator's plan for the eternal destiny of His children."

- ♥ "The divine plan of happiness enables family relationships to be perpetuated beyond the grave."

- ♥ "Sacred ordinances and covenants available in holy temples make it possible for individuals to return to the presence of God, and for families to be united eternally."

- ♥ "Husband and wife have a solemn responsibility to love and care for each other, and their children."

- ♥ "Parents have a sacred duty to rear their children in love and righteousness, . . . to teach them to love and serve one another . . . [and] will be held accountable before God for the discharge of these obligations."

- ♥ "Happiness in family life is most likely to be achieved when founded upon the teachings of the Lord Jesus Christ."

- ♥ "In these sacred responsibilities, fathers and mothers are obligated to help one another as equal partners."

- ♥ "Successful marriages and families are established and maintained on principles of faith, prayer, repentance, forgiveness, respect, love, compassion, work, and wholesome recreational activities."

4. Heed the expert advice of Church leaders.

♡ "No other success can compensate for failure in the home." (President David O. McKay, Conference Report, Apr. 1964, 5.)

♡ "The greatest work you will ever do will be within the walls of your own home." (*Teachings of Harold B. Lee,* 1996, 280.)

♡ "A successful parent is one who has loved, one who has sacrificed, and one who has cared for, taught, and ministered to the needs of a child. . . . My concern today is that there are parents who may be pronouncing harsh judgments upon themselves . . . when in fact they have done their best and should continue in faith." (President Howard W. Hunter, *Ensign,* Nov. 1983, 65.)

♡ "It is increasingly clear that we must teach the gospel to our families personally, live those teachings in our homes, or run the risk of discovering too late that a Primary teacher or priesthood adviser or seminary instructor *could* not do for our children what we *would* not do for them." (Elder Jeffrey R. Holland, *Ensign,* May 1983, 36; emphasis in original.)

♡ "In an eternal sense, salvation is a family affair. God holds parents responsible for their stewardship in rearing their family. It is a most sacred responsibility." (President Ezra Taft Benson, *Ensign,* July 1992, 2.)

♡ "There is no substitute for the home. Its foundation is as ancient as the world, and its mission has been ordained of God from the earliest times. . . . There can be no genuine happiness separate and apart from the home, and every effort made to sanctify and preserve its influence is uplifting to those who toil and sacrifice for its establishment. . . . There is no happiness without service, and there is no service greater than that which converts the home into a divine institution, and which promotes and preserves family life." (President Joseph F. Smith, *Gospel Doctrine,* 1939, 300.)

♥ "The home is what needs reforming. Try today, and tomorrow to make a change in your home by praying twice a day with your family. . . . Ask a blessing upon every meal you eat. Spend ten minutes . . . reading a chapter from the words of the Lord in the [scriptures]. . . . Let love, peace, and the Spirit of the Lord, kindness, charity, sacrifice for others, abound in your families. Banish harsh words, . . . and let the Spirit of God take possession of your hearts. Teach to your children these things, in spirit and power. . . . Not one child in a hundred would go astray, if the home environment, example and training, were in harmony with . . . the Gospel of Jesus Christ." (President Joseph F. Smith, *Gospel Doctrine,* 1939, 302.)

♥ "The shield of faith is to be made and fitted in the family. . . . The plan designed by the Father contemplates that man and woman, husband and wife, working together, fit each child individually with a shield of faith made to buckle on so firmly that it can neither be pulled off nor penetrated by those fiery darts. It takes the steady strength of a father to hammer out the metal of it and the tender hands of a mother to polish and fit it on. Sometimes one parent is left to do it alone. It is difficult, but it can be done. In the Church we can teach about the materials from which a shield of faith is made: reverence, courage, chastity, repentance, forgiveness, compassion. In church we can learn how to assemble and fit them together. But the actual making of and fitting on of the shield of faith belongs in the family circle. Otherwise it may loosen and come off in a crisis." (Elder Boyd K. Packer, *Ensign,* May 1995, 8.)

♡ "Home should be an anchor, a port in a storm, a refuge, a happy place in which to dwell, a place where we are loved and where we can love. . . . Home and family can be the center of one's earthly faith, where love and mutual responsibility are appropriately blended. Thinking of home with its pleasant and happy memories can make us stronger during our present and future days here upon the earth." (Elder Marvin J. Ashton, *Ensign,* Nov. 1992, 21.)

♡ "To any within the sound of my voice who may have [wayward] sons or daughters, may I suggest that you never quit trying. They are never lost until you have given up. Remember that it is love, more than any other thing, that will bring them back. Punishment is not likely to do it. Reprimands without love will not accomplish it. Patience, expressions of appreciation, and that strange and remarkable power which comes with prayer will eventually win through." (President Gordon B. Hinckley, *Ensign,* June 1985, 4.)

5. Follow the expert counsel in the scriptures.

♥ Read 1 Nephi 8. Ponder your role as a parent in bringing your family to the tree.

♥ Read Mosiah 1. Note that King Benjamin taught his own children before causing the tower to be built and speaking to the multitudes.

♥ Read the story of Helaman and the Stripling Warriors (Alma 53–58) and discover the secret weapon these young men possessed. Consider preparing your own family for battle.

♥ "And we talk of Christ, we rejoice in Christ, we preach of Christ, we prophesy of Christ, and we write according to our prophecies, that our children may know to what source they may look for a remission of their sins." (2 Ne. 25:26.)

♥ "And thou shalt love the Lord thy God with all thine heart, and with all thy soul, and with all thy might. And these words, which I command thee this day, shall be in thine heart: And thou shalt teach them diligently unto thy children, and shalt talk of them when thou sittest in thine house, and when thou walkest by the way, and when thou liest down, and when thou risest up." (Deut. 6:5–7.)

♥ "I have no greater joy than to hear that my children walk in truth." (3 John 1:4.)

♥ "And it is given unto [thy children] to know good from evil; . . . Wherefore teach . . . your children, that all men, everywhere, must repent, or they can in nowise inherit the kingdom of God, for no unclean thing can dwell there, or dwell in his presence. . . . Therefore I give unto you a commandment, to teach these things freely unto your children." (Moses 6:56–58.)

♡ "And all thy children shall be taught of the Lord; and great shall be the peace of thy children." (3 Ne. 22:13.)

♡ "Behold, I will send you Elijah the prophet before the coming of the great and dreadful day of the Lord: and he shall turn the heart of the fathers to the children, and the heart of the children to their fathers, lest I come and smite the earth with a curse." (Mal. 4:5–6.)

♡ "Establish a house, even a house of prayer, a house of fasting, a house of faith, a house of learning, a house of glory, a house of order, a house of God." (D&C 88:119.)

♡ "For this shall be a law unto the inhabitants of Zion, or in any of her stakes which are organized. . . . And they shall teach their children to pray, and to walk uprightly before the Lord." (D&C 68:26, 28.)

♡ "I have commanded you to bring up your children in light and truth. . . . Set in order [your] family, and see that they are more diligent and concerned at home, and pray always, or they shall be removed out of their place." (D&C 93:40, 50.)

♡ "Choose you this day whom ye will serve; . . . but as for me and my house, we will serve the Lord." (Josh. 24:15.)

6. Read inspired books on the subject of home and family.

- ♡ *Raising Up a Family to the Lord,* by Elder Gene R. Cook

- ♡ *Families,* a compilation of talks by LDS leaders

- ♡ *Functional Families,* by George D. Durrant

- ♡ *The Five Love Languages,* by Dr. Gary Chapman

- ♡ *Home with a Heart,* by Dr. James Dobson

- ♡ *Don't Sweat the Small Stuff with Your Family,* by Richard Carlson, Ph.D.

7. Listen to advice from grandparents on how to be good parents and grandparents.

Here are some suggestions from actual grandparents—those who know:

- ♡ "Love being a grandparent! Enjoy it, and let them know you do!"

- ♡ "Involvement is essential. You don't have to give them every moment of your life, but you ought to give them all you can."

- ♡ "Prayerfully consider how to be a blessing to your children and grandchildren."

- ♡ "Your role isn't to discipline the grandchildren—let the parents do it."

- ♡ "While your role isn't to discipline, you are still a teacher. Don't miss out on the opportunity to remain a great teacher for your children and grandchildren!"

♡ "Spend time with them, not because you have to, but because you want to—a healthy dose of both quantity and quality time. Spend one-on-one time."

♡ "When you are with them, express to them why you think they are so special, and more importantly, why they are important to you!"

♡ "Love them! Tell them!"

♡ "Hug them!"

♡ "Remember that you never stop being a parent or grandparent."

♡ "Love your grandchildren's parents as unconditionally as you love the grandchildren!"

♡ "Never, never, never, never play favorites!"

♡ "E-mail them."

♡ "Share your life with them through stories and pictures."

♡ "Be the family newsletter editor. Keep your family in touch by having a monthly newsletter."

♡ "Don't worry about leaving them money. Leave them a part of yourself."

♡ "Take each individual grandchild on their own trip, and have a purpose to it!"

♡ "Teach them the value of money. Emphasize their making good choices by giving money to be distributed to them at certain times in their lives, for example, upon graduation from high school or college."

♡ "Make their family a home evening kit, and have one of your own at your own home!"

♡ "Have them over for family night, or join them in their home sometimes. Have a monthly home evening for larger families."

♡ "Continue with traditions, remaining flexible for the families they now have on the other side, the in-laws."

♡ "Have lots of sleepovers with the grandkids."

♡ "Babysit for them sometimes. You don't want to be taken for granted, but do it because you *want* to, not because you *have* to!"

♡ "Be there at the crossroads of their lives. Support the things they are interested in, and attend things when you can."

♡ "Be a good listener."

♡ "Call and talk to them on the phone just to catch up. Your children and your grandchildren are busy, so you have to be the instigator."

♡ "Be a good example. You can't expect them to be something you are not."

♡ "Have special games or books or puzzles at your house for when they come. Keep special things in your purse or pocket to give them when you see them."

♡ "Give your grandkids a special nickname that shows love and affection—'my sunshine,' 'my buddy,' 'my princess,' 'my angel,' 'my man,' and so forth."

♡ "Share your testimony. Share it in spoken word, but also write it down!"

♡ "Write letters to your children and grandchildren—and not just while you are serving a mission. Plan to send letters or cards for holidays or special events to help you remember to keep up with each one and to ensure that they receive them consistently."

♡ "Keep a journal back and forth between you. Write something to them, and have them write something back to you. Mail it if necessary, but keep a dialogue going. It is fun to reread things you have written earlier."

♡ "Make a tradition out of giving the first missionary tie or the wedding veil, something that they can always cherish. For the younger ones, buy a handkerchief or necklace with their baptism date on it. Let them know you are proud of them and that you will always remember their good choices."

♡ "Make, purchase, or hand down blessing outfits."

♡ "Make a scrapbook or journal for them."

♡ "Get a 'Grandparent Remembers' book, and fill in all of the pages for them."

♡ "Share heirloom items and stories from ancestors. Be their link to the past. Try to save items from the past for them to cherish."

♡ "Have a prayer with them at the end of each visit. Pray vocally, expressing your gratitude for their life and how it enriches yours."

♡ "Have a secret password that belongs to just the two of you so that the child knows you will be a safe place in a time of trouble. Perhaps they will be out with friends and need a place to come to avoid evil influences. Or maybe mom and dad will become angry and the child will need a place to go and a tender heart to help them figure things out."

♡ "Every chance you get, express to them what great parents they have, and list specific reasons why."

♡ "Spend some time with your children and their spouses, doing things they love and care about."

♡ "Try to strike the delicate balance of being there for your children when they need you to be, and *not* when they don't. Respect their need to figure out some things on their own. Try to do the things you hoped your parents would do for you."

♡ "Never lose sight of what a privilege it is to be a parent. Never forget what an honor it is to be a grandparent."

♡ "Turn your hearts, in the ways the spirit of Elijah inspires you, to those who have gone before you and those who will come after you. Appreciate your heritage, and care about the ones you leave behind. Be the all-important link in the generations of your own personal family."

♡ "Forgive, as the father of the prodigal son did."

♡ "Don't concentrate on the past of your family life as much as you concentrate on what can be *now*, in the present! Maybe you didn't have family home evening as often as you should have. What can you do *now* to make up the difference? It isn't too late unless you give up."

♡ "Don't be overanxious. 'Worrying does not empty tomorrow of its troubles—it empties today of its strength.' Trust in him, and he will lead you."

♡ "Let your light so shine by your examples of love and service and testimony. What a wonderful blessing a grandparent is!"

♡ "Learn the love language of your children and grandchildren, and *love them, love them, love them!*"

8. Listen to expert parenting advice from children.

Again, here are some suggestions from those who know:

♡ "Listen to me when I am talking."

♡ "Don't yell at me when I do something wrong. I am not perfect."

♡ "Have confidence in me."

♡ "Believe that I can achieve my goals."

♡ "Say nice things when I'm crying."

♡ "Love me like you never loved anyone before."

♡ "Compliment me."

♡ "Be there for me."

♡ "Please try to be fair."

♡ "Remember when you were a kid."

♡ "Hold me when I am sad."

♡ "Be proud of my best."

♡ "Spend time with me."

♡ "Give me hugs and kisses."

♡ "Like my friends."

♡ "Don't let your frustration show too much. I don't want to disappoint you."

♡ "Play with me sometimes."

♡ "Help me with my homework."

♡ "Teach me about Jesus."

9. Listen to expert advice from the voice of inspiration.

Elder Henry B. Eyring said, "Our families can be given a gift to know what God would have them do and to learn it in a way that will encourage them to do it." (*Ensign,* May 1996, 62.) He also said, "We can expect that God won't just tell us a few interesting things about the family; he will tell us what a family ought to be and why. Further, we know that our Heavenly Father and his Son, Jesus Christ, want us to become like them so that we can dwell with them forever in families. . . . As we read what the proclamation tells us about the family, we can expect—in fact, we must expect—impressions to come to our minds as to what we are to do. And we can be confident it is possible for us to do according to those impressions." (*Ensign,* Feb. 1998, 10.)

We can be sure that Heavenly Father will give us guidance when it comes to raising our families. Who better than he to know about your family and what your family needs? Pray for inspiration. No expert advice will be greater.

10. Trust your own heart.

When it comes to *your* family, your heart is an expert. Who could possibly love your child more than you—their parent? Who could have fonder desires, greater hopes, and better-thought-through dreams for the future of your family members than you? Every parent is blessed with God-given instincts to tap into. Every parent is blessed with a capacity worth increasing. Every parent is blessed with a love that has a full potential. When you have *sincerely* sought the guidance of the Holy Ghost, and you are doing what you do out of love, you can trust your own heart to guide you.

SUMMARY

You can always know that our Heavenly Father will send inspiration for your family to help you to face the storms of life—and to help you make the most of the sunny days of life. He has blessed you with "experts," ranging from ancient to modern-day prophets to the little child, who can lead you. (See 2 Ne. 21:6.) Heavenly Father cares so much about you and your family that he will not leave you to wander alone. In 1 Nephi 17:13 it says, "And I will also be your light in the wilderness; and I will prepare the way before you, if it so be that ye shall keep my commandments; wherefore, inasmuch as ye shall keep my commandments ye shall be led towards the promised land; and ye shall know that it is by me that ye are led." As you keep his commandments, he *will* lead you, whether it be by his own voice, the voice of his servants (see D&C 1:38), or the loving voice of children, expert grandparents, or the Holy Ghost. He will lead you, and you will know that it is by him that you are led.

25
KEEP A HEALTHY PERSPECTIVE

"And see that all these things are done in wisdom and order; for it is not requisite that a man should run faster than he has strength. And again, it is expedient that he should be diligent, that thereby he might win the prize; therefore, all things must be done in order."

Mosiah 4:27

Keep a Healthy Perspective

1. Give it *time*.

"Rome wasn't built in a day," the saying goes. You don't have to change the world overnight, or even your own little corner of it. It is tough to be patient, but your efforts will be rewarded. Keep in mind that life is a journey. You will know by whom you have been led, and you will taste of the sweetness of his rewards.

2. Give it *sincerity*.

We don't need to be scholars or highly skilled technicians to testify of Heavenly Father's love. We only need to believe it, mean it, and give the best we have. When we do so with a sincere heart, he will magnify our efforts, and we will succeed.

3. Give it *love*.

Let your efforts testify of him who loves you. Do your best because you love him. Give it your best because you love your family. Let love be the driving force in each and every effort, attempt, and thought. You will find that love is the greatest single motivator of all.

4. Give it *a realistic perspective*.

Set a reachable standard. No one is perfect. You will make mistakes. Your children will make mistakes. It isn't healthy to set your expectations too high. You can be hopeful and realistic at the same time. Perfection is in the practice!

5. Give it *balance and strength*.

Nothing wonderful ever happened without effort. Be strong. It may not be easy, but there are simple steps you can take without hesitation or fear. Heavenly Father's advice is to do things in wisdom and order. Don't run faster than you have strength, but be diligent that you might win the prize. (See Mosiah 4:27.)

6. Give it *an eternal perspective*.

There is more to life than the time we know on this earth. Strive to think of the grander picture. Eternity is at stake when we make decisions for our families. Consider your knowledge of who we are, why we are here, and where we are going. Each question has an eternal answer that will help you keep this earth life in perspective.

7. Give it *optimism*.

Look on the sunny side, and you will find yourself there. When you look at your tasks to accomplish and the connections you want to make with your family, recognize those things as a gift and a privilege, instead of a burden and a restriction. Keep your eye on the doughnut, not on the hole. Be positive and optimistic; great joys will follow.

8. Give it *laughter*.

There are times when you might as well laugh. It's okay that the kids are rolling over the furniture or starting up wrestling matches during family night. Go ahead and enjoy their spirit and spontaneity. It takes more muscles to frown than smile, and laughter *is* the best medicine.

9. Give yourself a *break!*

You love your family, and you want what is best for them. You read this book, didn't you? Give yourself a pat on the back for all of your good efforts and recognize that you don't have to be all things to all people at all times (even though it feels that way sometimes!). Don't let yourself get overwhelmed or feel guilty at perceived short-comings. We all think that everyone else has it more together than we do. The simple truth is that they usually don't. We all have good days, and we all, unfortunately, have bad days.

Give yourself a round of applause (and keep up the good work!).

10. Give the rest to *God.*

Your best is really amazing. When you consider that you are his child, created in his image, you have a lot to give. Be confident that with his help all things are possible. When Abraham Lincoln was questioned about being frightened by threats of an assassin's bullet, he said, "I must do my duty as I see it, and leave the rest with God!" Do what you know you can do, and leave the rest with your loving Heavenly Father. Do your duty as you see it, and then take him at his word when he says, "Be still and know that I am God." (D&C 101:16.)

SUMMARY

An appropriate perspective can change what we perceive in our minds, what we feel in our hearts, and even how we see with our eyes. There may be things that cloud your vision or create a blind spot, even an obstacle that blocks your view. How much simpler life would be if we could view the present with hindsight, or had 20/20 vision all the time. What if we had the ability to foresee the future?

The truth of it is, there are certain obstacles or clouds that limit our vision from time to time. Often we are kept from seeing the truth or the reality of our circumstances by a lack of perspective. Far too often, we create our own limitations with feelings of inadequacy, excuses, or even indifference. These blinders can block our vision of who we are, what our mission is, and what we are capable of doing.

Heavenly Father has given us everything we need to keep the right perspective. He wants us to feel like the strong, capable individuals he created. He wants us to tap into the power that comes from a personal relationship with him. He wants us to trust him and believe in ourselves. He wants us to let go of the past, and take hold of the present and the future. He wants each of us to have a clear, happy, hopeful perspective that is free of the weight of sin, fear, or pride. And he can heal the blindness we create for ourselves.

In short, he wants us to utilize the Atonement in raising our families. He will help you to do what matters most, for the people who matter most to you, as you diligently seek him. May his choicest blessings be upon you as you believe deeply and actively in your family!

EPILOGUE

A few short years ago, after enjoying great Chinese food with my husband and some friends, I enthusiastically opened the fortune cookie. I have never believed in cookie fortunes, but have always been amused by them. This one was no exception. I laughed when I read it—but I didn't toss it back on to the plate to be thrown away by the waitress. Instead, I tucked it into my pocket, and to this day it remains mounted on my computer monitor.

The "fortune" said, "You are a lover of words; someday you will write a book." It was funny to me because I didn't consider myself a writer, nor did I think I knew any subject well enough to write an entire book. But it was also intriguing, because I guess deep down I knew this particular fortune actually fit me. I *am* a lover of words. And my "someday" arrived when the opportunity to write this book presented itself. Although I have felt like I have been on the steepest and fastest of roller coasters throughout this process, I have never at any point felt that I have been alone on this ride—not when I decided to take the risk and write a book ("lover" of words doesn't necessarily equal "skilled" with words), not on any uphill climb as I struggled with some of the details of writing, and not when the book was finished. God has said he will not leave us alone, and he truly keeps all of his promises.

Not only do I have a love for words, but I have two all-encompassing, soul-fulfilling passions in my life. One passion is for the knowledge of a loving Heavenly Father, and his atoning Son,

Jesus Christ. The other passion is for "family," all of yours, and especially mine. Sharing these passions with you and bearing witness of our obligations to both is truly an honor and a privilege.

I hope that as you have read this book, you have felt comfort in knowing of God's gifts to families—especially to yours—and that you, too, have felt that you are not alone in the process.

Having you know my name means nothing to me. Having you know of my witness means everything to me. My having received the gift of this inspiration and the opportunity to share that inspiration does not make me important. It is the message that is important.

I want the life I have led to be a legacy of testimony and of love. If there is a "mark" to be left on this world, I pray that mark will be about those two all-encompassing, soul-fulfilling great loves in my life—my testimony and my family. It is also my goal to live just like the tenth leper: aware of my innumerable blessings, knowing the Source, and giving thanks and credit where credit is due.

May you also experience the blessings, know the Source, and find joy as you leave your family your own legacy of testimony and love.